HOW TO CHOOSE THE RIGHT CAREER

HOW TO CHOOSE THE RIGHT CAREER

Louise Welsh Schrank

Printed on recyclable paper

VGM Career Horizons
a division of *NTC Publishing Group*
Lincolnwood, Illinois USA

Acknowledgments

Data and descriptions in the Career Finder were developed by the U.S. Department of Labor.

Rena Trevor and students in the Harper College Career Development Program were supportive in field testing materials for this book.

Special thanks to Barbara Wood Donner for her assistance in the preparation of this revised edition.

1997 Printing

Published by VGM Career Horizons, a division of NTC Publishing Group.
© 1991 by NTC Publishing Group, 4255 West Touhy Avenue,
Lincolnwood (Chicago), Illinois 60646-1975 U.S.A.
All rights reserved. No part of this book may be reproduced, stored
in a retrieval system, or transmitted in any form or by any means,
electronic, mechanical, photocopying, recording or otherwise, without
prior permission of NTC Publishing Group.
Library of Congress Catalog Card No.: 91-65382
Manufactured in the United States of America.

7 8 9 VP 9 8 7 6

Contents

Introduction ix

Part I: Awareness and Exploration

1. Your Dream Job 3
Exploring Your "Shoulds" 4
I Won't Feel I've Really Lived Unless... 6

2. Your Favorite People 8
Your Group at the Party 9

3. Your Needs 13
Levels of Development 13
Self-Actualization 15

4. The Interest Indicator 17
Interest/Skill Intersections 19
What Kind of Work Do You Like Best? 19

5. Skill Identification 27
Relating Your Skills to Desirable Careers 36

6. Job Characteristics 40

7. Rewards and Satisfactions 44

8 Getting Field Experience 50
Getting Experience through Volunteer and Part-time Work 51

9 The Advice Interview 59

10 Research a Career 62

11 The Composite Picture 65

12 The Career Finder 67
25 Common Job Skills and Characteristics 69

Part II: Developing a Game Plan

13 Your Educational and Career Alternatives 107

14 Possible Training Programs and College Majors 110
The Body Workers 111
The Data Detail 113
The Persuaders 114
The Service Workers 114
The Creative Artists 115
The Investigators 116

15 Choosing a College 117
Should You Choose a Large School or a Small School? 119
Other Factors to Consider when Choosing a College 120
Which College Major Is Best? 121
Should You Join the Military? 122

16 Choosing a Vocational School 124
Consumer's Guide to Vocational Schools 125

17 Consider an Apprenticeship 127

18 Consider Correspondence Schools, Cooperative Programs, and On-the-Job Training 132
Correspondence and Television Schools 132
Cooperative Programs 133
On-the-Job Training Programs 134

19 Predict the Results 135

20 Overcome Your Barriers 137
Take a Risk Today 138
The "I Can'ts" 139
The "You Can'ts" (Other People's Expectations) 139

21 Summarize Your Information 141
Breakthrough Plans 142
Decision Wrap-Up 143

Part III: Marketing Yourself

22 A Consumer's Guide to Job Search Strategies 147
Networking 148
Newspaper Ads 152
Employment Agencies 155
School Placement Offices 156

23 Resumes, Applications, and Cover Letters 158
A Step-by-Step Guide for Resume Preparation 158

Rules for Resume Writing 159
Correspondence That Wins
　Interviews 168
Application Forms 170

24 The Interview 173
Interview Strategy No. 1: Winning
　Interviews 173
Your Legal Rights 176
Interview Strategy No. 2: Know Your
　Rights 176
Assertive Interviewing
　Techniques 180
Check Your Body Language 180
Investigate the Employer 181
Rehearsing the Interview 184
The Questions Behind the
　Questions 184
Winning the Salary Game 186

25 Checklist for Winning the Employment Game 189

26 Career Planning in a Changing World 192
Life Changes That Can Affect Career
　and Life Planning 193

Related Reading 195

Introduction

The ladder was long used as a metaphor to symbolize the progress of a career. People were supposed to climb their career ladders in one direction. In considering how best to develop a life plan, we would like to suggest another metaphor—the Scandinavian *parcours*. The *parcours* is an exercise trail with a set of planned stops where people exercise and develop different muscles or facets of themselves.

A career plan is like a *parcours* where people can travel through several different occupations or stops along life's path. People today can plan ahead, knowing that they will likely have different careers that will develop or actualize different skills, needs, and values.

Self-assessment, goal determination, and decision making need to be done at different junctures while traveling the *parcours* of life. People need to decide on goals and a direction as they begin their travel on the *parcours* during the first phase of adulthood, and perhaps several more times during their lives. The exercises in this book are designed to help you decide what your next life-style should be, and to be aware that life and career planning do not end with your first choice. Everyone reaches points in life when they need to rethink, and possibly rechart, their direction in life. They need to push on to new and more challenging stops in the *parcours*.

Life changes, like increasing or decreasing responsibilities to others, changing financial responsibilities, and maturing interests often propel people to find work different from what they originally thought they would do. Many people want to retool for a second or a third career. They may want new training to update and extend educations they obtained when they were younger. This book has proven to be a useful tool to thousands of men and women reentering the job market or seeking a new career.

The image of the career plan as a series of stops on the *parcours* also applies to other situations. People who work in declining industries are forced to reassess themselves and chart new courses. Discouragement or boredom are other reasons people look for changes. The open-ended exercises in *How to Choose the Right Career* are just as meaningful for people with years of experience in the work force as for people with little experience.

By choosing to work with this book, you have taken a positive step in determining your future. *How to Choose the Right Career* provides an opportunity and a structure for a systematic search for the right career. You are beginning a process that will enable you to *plan* your future rather than settle for the first thing that comes along.

Using this Book
Part I: awareness and exploration

The exercises in this book are appropriate for people who are exploring career options. The process is useful for all ages: exploration of the self, exploration of the working world, acquisition of the right education, marketing yourself to gain the right job.

How to Choose the Right Career begins with an exploration of your skills, needs, and values. The best career decisions begin with you—who you are, your strengths, your weaknesses. With good self-understanding you can begin to relate to the career options available.

Many people do not really recognize what talents they would be happiest using in their work. Few can readily identify which of their needs must be met if they are to enjoy their work lives. Since work takes up a great deal of time—usually about two thousand hours a year for 40-50 years—the motivation to find something you would like doing should be strong.

As a workbook, *How to Choose the Right Career* is only half written. The part that is not written is about you. The charts, activities, and projects provide an easy-to-follow system to help you discover and assemble information about yourself that can be applied to available jobs. This process can lead to recognition of the kinds of work that can bring you personal happiness and fulfillment. There are many "good" careers, but the real value of any career depends on what it does for the person who pursues it—if it has a growing future and uses the person's talents.

How to Choose the Right Career can be used individually or in group sessions. It can help the professional career counselor or the individual career seeker to analyze and understand interests, aptitudes, and values. By using this book's procedure of self-understanding, research, and advice interviews, you can become your own excellent career counselor.

An extensive, 20-page Career Finder starting on page 67 lists several hundred job titles, some of which will probably be entirely new to you. It charts specific job characteristics associated with these occupations to help you relate your self-understanding to the working world. The Career Finder is an exploratory tool which will help you evaluate your interests, preferences, and qualifications for the jobs available.

The Career Finder can help you identify appropriate careers for you. Formal vocational testing, available in schools and career counseling services, can supplement and refine the direction your career plan should take.

Part II: developing a game plan

Once you have formulated a career objective, you will need to develop a plan of action. Many people will want more training and education to achieve their desired career. Many promising careers begin with training at community colleges or vocational schools, as well as four-year colleges or universities. *How to Choose the Right Career* can help you select a career with educational qualifications you can achieve, whether through short-term vocational training or long-term college work.

Part III: marketing yourself

Marketing yourself is the final phase in developing a career plan. Steps in marketing include developing an effective resume or application form, scouting the available jobs, and interviewing effectively. How well you market yourself during your job search will largely determine how easily you can land the job you want. The final chapters of this book deal with these elements of selling an employer on hiring you.

Part I

AWARENESS AND EXPLORATION

Your Dream Job   1

To find best clues to careers that will bring you happiness, you should begin with your own imagination. Imagine that you can be anything you want to be, disregarding the necessary qualifications, talents, or money needed to do it. If you could have any job that you wanted in the whole world, what would that job be? Visualize yourself in that job, and hold the image in your mind.

As children, people usually have many ideas about what they want to be. But as they grow older, responsibilities arise. Many people drift into occupations more by chance, or need for a job, than by choice. When they reach middle life, they often regret not following the dreams of their youth.

So, why not begin the process of creating your new life plan by closing your eyes and imagining your dream job. Picture yourself at work in as much detail as possible. What are you doing? Where do you work? How much do you earn? Spend several minutes or longer conjuring up your fantasy job. When you are finished, note the main details on the lines below. On a separate sheet of paper write a description, and/or draw a picture of how you see yourself in your special job. Next, ask yourself how you can make part or all of this dream job come true.

_____

_____

_____

_____

_____

_____

Exploring Your "Shoulds"

Far too many people never follow their own dreams. Their occupational choices are often shaped by what other people think they should do.

"You *should* go to college."

"You *should* serve your country."

"You *should* earn a lot of money."

"You *should* be a lawyer (a doctor, or a teacher) because your parent or your grandparent was."

Many people spend their whole lives doing just what *others* think they should do, rather than what *they* want to do. They are tyrannized by the "shoulds" of their parents, teachers, friends, social class, and other role models.

The chart below will help you to evaluate the importance of some other people's expectations on your career choices. On the scale of one to ten, mark an X to indicate the degree of importance of each person's opinions and influence over you. (1 = little influence, 2 = great influence.)

INFLUENCE	1	2	3	4	5	6	7	8	9	10
Father										
Mother										
Mate										
Brother										
Sister										
Children										
Boyfriend/girlfriend										
Close friends										
Religious leader										
Teacher										
Counselor										
Others										

On a separate piece of paper, list the strongest "shoulds" that have been imposed on you by others. Which are the "shoulds" that really matter to you? List them below.

I should _____

I should _____

I should _____

I should _____

I should _____

These feelings, beliefs, or values will have some weight in your career choices, but they should be balanced and considered along with others that you hold.

Who "should" hold what job

Being female or male has long imposed many "shoulds" that may not be realistic at all. Some people feel that men should hold jobs that demand physical strength or management of money and people. Women should perform nurturing work—an extension of their mothering role. Jobs with titles like teacher, nurse, or beautician have until rather recently been considered by many people to be "woman's work."

Today, almost all careers in the United States are legally open to both men and women. Yet many people still feel uncomfortable at the thought of performing certain jobs because of their sex. A woman might feel that engineering or construction jobs are closed to her. A man might feel that he could not get hired as a nurse, a secretary, a primary school teacher, or a beautician.

If you are male, try to think of a traditionally "female" job you might like to hold. If you are female, try to think of a traditionally "male" job you would find attractive. Explain why you think you would like the job.

_____
_____
_____
_____

I Won't Feel I've Really Lived Unless...

Career planning concerns your life's *mission,* or what you see the meaning of your life to be. Think about the most important life's work for you. Then finish this statement in as many ways as you can. I won't feel I've really lived unless....

_____
_____
_____
_____
_____
_____
_____

Naturally, many of the things you want to do in your lifetime have nothing to do with the world of work, but many of them probably could be part of a job.

Think over the items on your list. Now go back and draw a circle around any of your dreams which could be accomplished by a satisfying paid career.

Your Favorite People 2

Another way to discover clues to good choices of work is to think of the relationships you will form on the job. If you like the people you work with, you will be more likely to enjoy the work you are doing. People are often attracted to people who have interests and skills similar to their own. The following exercises help to identify the kinds of people you like best, and relate your preferences to the working world. You can begin to recognize the type of person you would like to work with by thinking of specific people you have known. Try to state your reasons for liking and disliking them.

I like people who . . .

_____

_____

_____

I do not like people who . . .

_____

_____

_____

Describe the kinds of people you would like to work with:

_____

_____

_____

Your Group at the Party

Suppose you were at a party where guests were grouped according to their interests. Suppose you would have enough time to mingle with people in only two of the groups described on this page and the next. Which group would you pick first? Which second?

1. *The Body Workers*:
   These people enjoy physical activity, work with their hands, or heavy work requiring strength and endurance. They may need special clothing for their work and may be dirty or physically exhausted at the end of their work day. Body workers often work with objects, machines, plants, or animals, and they often like to work outdoors.

2. *The Data Detail*:
   These people use numbers or words in their work in very exact ways. They know that being attentive to detail is important, and they like to work without

errors. They often have good clerical or math abilities.

3. *The Persuaders*:
Persuaders like to work and talk with people and enjoy convincing others to see things their way. Persuaders often work in sales, law, or politics, where their success is measured by how well they influence others.

4. *The Service Workers*:
Service workers find their job satisfaction in helping others. They often work in schools, hospitals, or social service agencies, as teachers, nurses, or counselors.

5. *The Creative Artists*:
Creative artists are people who express themselves through music, dance, drama, writing, or art. Many creative artists can only afford to work at their chosen jobs part-time because demand (and pay) for many creative workers' jobs is low. They may earn all or part of their income by working in related areas where their creativity, knowledge, and skill are utilized in at least part of the work.

6. *The Investigators*:
Investigators enjoy asking the questions *Why?* and *How?* in their work. They work with scientific or technical information, applying it to new situations. They may work in scientific research or analysis as well as applications.

Which group of people would you instinctively be drawn to most and enjoy being with for the longest time?

_____

After half an hour, if you had to move, what group would you choose second?

_____

Most jobs fit into one of, or a combination of, the categories described in the party exercise above. Each group attracts different kinds of co-workers and involves a different kind of work. The Career Finder on pages 67–104 codes each occupation into one of these occupational groups:

I.	Body Workers	Often including athletes, physical instructors, and "blue collar" workers, these people work with tools or machines in skilled trades, outdoor, technical, or service jobs. Body workers are typically practical, rugged, athletic, healthy, and aggressive.
II.	Data Detail	Part of the "white collar" or office workers, these people hold jobs involving clerical or numerical tasks, such as banking, bookkeeping, data processing, and accounting. These workers are usually good at following instructions and attending carefully to detail work.
III.	Persuaders	Usually holding management or sales positions, these workers have jobs where they persuade people to perform some kind of action, such as buying goods and services.
IV.	Service Workers	Often working in education, health care, or social welfare, these workers hold jobs where they teach, heal, or help people. Hair dressers, waiters, instructors, health care workers, and tour guides are part of this group.
V.	Creative Artists	These people work with words, music, or art in a creative way. Actors, musicians, composers, authors, and sculptors are in this group.
VI.	Investigators	Usually performing scientific or laboratory work, investigators research how the world is put together and how to solve problems.

To which group would a worker doing your dream job (described on page 4) belong? For example, if your dream job is to be a movie star, a person with that job would probably be found in group V, Creative Artists.

My fantasy job belongs to group ____, or a combination of groups ____ and ____.

Is the group to which your fantasy job belongs the same as one of the groups you selected in the party exercise? If so, this is a strong indication that your greatest work satisfaction may be found in a career in that category.

Your Needs 3

Levels of Development

Psychologist Abraham Maslow studied the relationship between needs and motivation for many years and suggested that it is our needs that motivate the way we act. He developed a hierarchy of needs which he diagrammed as a pyramid, showing five levels of needs that motivate human beings.

- Level 1 is *Survival.* At this most basic level, we strive for food, clothing, and shelter—our basic needs to stay alive.

- At Level 2 is *Safety.* At this level, people strive for more security—savings, insurance, safe working places, safe homes and communities.

- Level 3 is *Belongingness.* To achieve belongingness, people work for good relationships with their families and friends, co-workers, and groups in their communities.

- Level 4 is *Esteem*. At this level, people may strive for recognition and respect in their life's work and in the community at large. At work, they may seek more autonomy, the right to schedule their own time, and take more responsibility.

- Level 5 is *Self-Actualization*. At this highest level, the individual strives for the highest development of personal potential, including the establishment and fulfillment of individual goals, the ongoing growth of personal freedom, creativity, responsibility, mastery of skills and accomplishment that is valued by oneself and one's family, friends, and community.

Many people work to achieve the basic needs of Levels 1 and 2. These needs must be fulfilled before the higher level needs can concern a person greatly. If a person has enough income, basic needs can be met. A person's work also enables her or him to be with other people and to maintain a family, thus fulfilling at least part of the Level 3 need for belonging.

As a person begins to fulfill needs in Level 4, work takes on more importance. It becomes important to develop a sense of confidence and achievement in one's life. For many people, their sense of self-esteem comes from their work.

Once the first four levels of needs have been largely fulfilled, a person craves self-actualization. This deals with the concept of having a mission in life. This need causes some independently wealthy people to continue to work. Work brings more than just money as a reward.

Consider your own feelings about these needs, and record some of your thoughts in notes on the lines below.

At this time in your life, what level need do you think motivates you the most? _____

_____

_____

_____

What are some of the ways that you might fulfill your own levels of needs in the future? Write down one or two ideas next to each level listed below.

Level 1 (Survival): _____

_____

Level 2 (Safety): _____

_____

Level 3 (Belongingness): _____

_____

Level 4 (Esteem): _____

_____

Level 5 (Self-Actualization): _____

_____

Self-Actualization   Choose two or three people in positions of leadership or in your community about whom you have substantial information. You could choose a successful teacher, religious leader, businessperson, family member, or neighbor. Think over the levels on which these people have developed their lives. Remember that to be self-actualizing, the person does not have to be rich or famous; the person may be recognized and valued within a particular family or community.

When you have chosen two or three possibilities, write in their names on the next page, and think over how they have fulfilled their needs at Levels 1, 2, 3, 4, and 5. Consider how some of their choices and methods would work out for you. Would you choose some of the same actions? Which ones would be of value to you, as you plan your own career and life-style?

Person #1: _____

_____

_____

_____

_____

_____

_____

Person #2: _____

_____

_____

_____

_____

_____

_____

Person #3: _____

_____

_____

_____

_____

_____

_____

The Interest Indicator 4

Identifying things that you like to do can help you find a potentially satisfying career. If you enjoy your work, you can do it better. Recognizing what kinds of work give you pleasure is a key clue in finding a good occupational "fit."

The following Interest Indicator Sheet will give you a chance to rate the pleasure you get from some of your activities.

By examining the experiences that you liked, and that you didn't like, you can get clues to good career directions.

Think of experiences that you have really enjoyed. Was it getting a new puppy? Helping your grandmother in her garden? Helping paint apartments last summer with your uncle? Whatever you can think of that really made you feel good is something worth considering. The things that you enjoy, that are special to you, may provide you with the best clues to the kinds of work you can be good at, and enjoy the most.

18 *How to Choose the Right Career*

Interest Indicator Sheet

On the numbered lines below, list 10 activities you have enjoyed doing in the past four years. Include special school projects, extracurricular activities, hobbies, summer and after-school activities, volunteer or paid work activities. Read the statements above each column and put a check in the square for each activity on your list about which the statement is true.

Think of activities that you have done that other people have not done, as well as the more ordinary ones.

	This activity involves some kind of risk—financial, physical, or emotional.	This activity gives you a joyful feeling.	You believe this activity will help you grow as a person.	You spend more than $3 each time you do this activity.	You would like to let others know that you do this.	You spent at least four hours each week in the last month.	You spend time reading, thinking, or worrying about this activity.	You consciously choose this over other possible activities.
1.								
2.								
3.								
4.								
5.								
6.								
7.								
8.								
9.								
10.								

Interest/Skill Intersections

Select the top five activities from your Interest Indicator Sheet according to the number of marks next to each item—the activity with the most marks being first. List these top five interests in the column to the left, below.

In the middle column, list challenges that are related to each interest. What must you know how to do in order to complete that kind of task well? In the column to the right, list skills you will want to develop further.

INTERESTS	CHALLENGES	SKILLS TO DEVELOP FURTHER
(sample) Design bulletin board display	Work requiring self-expression	Lettering skills
1.		
2.		
3.		
4.		
5.		

What Kind of Work Do You Like Best?

The lists on the following pages describe activities performed in many different occupations. You can use them to identify the kinds of work you like. Read each job listed and determine your interest in it. Don't consider salary, status, or necessary education. Consider only how good you feel when you visualize yourself doing the job.

For each item decide the degree of your interest in the activity. Circle the number describing your interest as shown below. Do this on each of the six pages which follow.

⓪ 1 2 3   Not interested. Would detest doing this work.

0 ① 2 3   Slightly interested. Would do it if you had to.

0 1 ② 3   Interested. You would enjoy doing this work.

0 1 2 ③   Extremely interested. You would love a job where you could perform this activity.

Interest Indicator
Group I: The Body Workers

	Not interested	Slightly interested	Interested	Extremely interested
1. Move furniture	0	1	2	3
2. Trim bushes and trees	0	1	2	3
3. Be a dancer	0	1	2	3
4. Assemble automobile engines	0	1	2	3
5. Farm land and tend farm animals	0	1	2	3
6. Teach skiing	0	1	2	3
7. Coach athletics	0	1	2	3
8. Install electrical wiring	0	1	2	3
9. Repair and paint houses	0	1	2	3
10. Pack and ship goods	0	1	2	3
11. Be a forest ranger	0	1	2	3
12. Be a lumberjack	0	1	2	3
13. Work in a furniture factory	0	1	2	3
14. Build houses	0	1	2	3
15. Drive a large truck	0	1	2	3
16. Install water heaters	0	1	2	3
17. Park cars at a parking lot	0	1	2	3
18. Teach fitness classes	0	1	2	3
19. Lay brick for new buildings	0	1	2	3
20. Be a lifeguard	0	1	2	3
21. Run a bulldozer	0	1	2	3
22. Repair faulty plumbing	0	1	2	3
23. Captain a ship	0	1	2	3
24. Be a dockworker	0	1	2	3
25. Be a professional baseball player	0	1	2	3
TOTALS				

Interest Indicator
Group II: The Data Detail

	Not interested	Slightly interested	Interested	Extremely interested
1. Connect long-distance telephone calls	0	1	2	3
2. Make travel reservations	0	1	2	3
3. Review credit applications	0	1	2	3
4. Estimate cost of repairing damaged autos	0	1	2	3
5. Collect money from customers and make change	0	1	2	3
6. Proofread type for publication	0	1	2	3
7. Shelve books at a library	0	1	2	3
8. Duplicate printed materials	0	1	2	3
9. File records and correspondence	0	1	2	3
10. Run a FAX machine	0	1	2	3
11. Serve as a data-processing keypunch operator	0	1	2	3
12. Assist doctors with office work	0	1	2	3
13. Keep records of business transactions	0	1	2	3
14. Enter insurance claims onto the computer	0	1	2	3
15. Do typing and word processing	0	1	2	3
16. Count, sort, and store supplies for inventories	0	1	2	3
17. Record court proceedings	0	1	2	3
18. Take shorthand and type letters	0	1	2	3
19. Sort mail	0	1	2	3
20. Estimate costs and buy business materials	0	1	2	3
21. Prepare financial and tax reports	0	1	2	3
22. Operate business machines	0	1	2	3
23. Maintain payroll records	0	1	2	3
24. Keep detailed records of payments and sales	0	1	2	3
25. Write business letters	0	1	2	3
TOTALS				

Interest Indicator
Group III: The Persuaders

	Not interested	Slightly interested	Interested	Extremely interested
1. Sell life and health insurance	0	1	2	3
2. Explain the company's wage and salary plans to employees	0	1	2	3
3. Sell automobiles to customers	0	1	2	3
4. Recruit workers for a business	0	1	2	3
5. Sell merchandise across a counter in a store	0	1	2	3
6. Manage a sales force	0	1	2	3
7. Demonstrate products like food, appliances, and gadgets	0	1	2	3
8. Sell aluminum siding to home owners	0	1	2	3
9. Manage a hotel or store	0	1	2	3
10. Help people transact business in a bank	0	1	2	3
11. Serve as head of a hospital	0	1	2	3
12. Appraise real estate value	0	1	2	3
13. Work as a lawyer at trials	0	1	2	3
14. Interview possible employees	0	1	2	3
15. Act in commercials on radio or TV	0	1	2	3
16. Manage a gas station	0	1	2	3
17. Buy grains at a commodity exchange	0	1	2	3
18. Run a floral shop	0	1	2	3
19. Serve meals and drinks on an airplane	0	1	2	3
20. Guide travelers on European tours	0	1	2	3
21. Direct recreation programs at park district	0	1	2	3
22. Manage an apartment building	0	1	2	3
23. Judge trials and legal proceedings	0	1	2	3
24. Argue legal matters before a jury	0	1	2	3
25. Contract for building materials and labor	0	1	2	3
TOTALS				

Interest Indicator
Group IV: The Service Workers

	Not interested	Slightly interested	Interested	Extremely interested
1. Interview welfare clients	0	1	2	3
2. Serve as a nurse in a hospital	0	1	2	3
3. Coach a children's athletic team	0	1	2	3
4. Help people who are poor or in trouble	0	1	2	3
5. Be a Peace Corps worker	0	1	2	3
6. Attend to the spiritual needs of people	0	1	2	3
7. Teach history in a high school	0	1	2	3
8. Plan meals and diets for elderly people	0	1	2	3
9. Seat customers at a restaurant	0	1	2	3
10. Teach children in a nursery school	0	1	2	3
11. Direct funerals	0	1	2	3
12. Help keep law and order in a community	0	1	2	3
13. Be a representative in a state legislature	0	1	2	3
14. Manage a home for your own family	0	1	2	3
15. Serve as a fire fighter in a fire department	0	1	2	3
16. Be a doctor	0	1	2	3
17. Teach crafts in a community center	0	1	2	3
18. Raise children	0	1	2	3
19. Give manicures	0	1	2	3
20. Be a waiter or waitress	0	1	2	3
21. Be in charge of a community library	0	1	2	3
22. Clean teeth and teach dental hygiene	0	1	2	3
23. Advise people who want to make career choices	0	1	2	3
24. Care for elderly people in a retirement home	0	1	2	3
25. Teach handicapped children	0	1	2	3
TOTALS				

Interest Indicator
Group V: The Creative Artists

	Not interested	Slightly interested	Interested	Extremely interested
1. Act in plays	0	1	2	3
2. Draw comics or animated films	0	1	2	3
3. Plan public relations for a political candidate	0	1	2	3
4. Perform as a singer or dancer before an audience	0	1	2	3
5. Teach literature in a college	0	1	2	3
6. Write stories or books about people and places	0	1	2	3
7. Conduct an orchestra	0	1	2	3
8. Play in a band or orchestra	0	1	2	3
9. Paint pictures	0	1	2	3
10. Design and draw plans for buildings	0	1	2	3
11. Photograph people and events	0	1	2	3
12. Review movies for a newspaper	0	1	2	3
13. Design interiors for homes or stores	0	1	2	3
14. Direct a community theater	0	1	2	3
15. Paint posters for stores	0	1	2	3
16. Do layout for a magazine	0	1	2	3
17. Set up displays in store windows	0	1	2	3
18. Teach art in a high school	0	1	2	3
19. Design furniture	0	1	2	3
20. Write radio program scripts	0	1	2	3
21. Edit books	0	1	2	3
22. Teach dancing	0	1	2	3
23. Interpret foreign languages	0	1	2	3
24. Create sculptures	0	1	2	3
25. Design fashions	0	1	2	3
TOTALS				

Interest Indicator
Group VI: The Investigators

	Not interested	Slightly interested	Interested	Extremely interested
1. Study, care for, and protect animals' health	0	1	2	3
2. Take X-ray photographs at a hospital	0	1	2	3
3. Study and search for uses of atomic energy	0	1	2	3
4. Study the way human beings behave	0	1	2	3
5. Check and control a county's water supply	0	1	2	3
6. Design and construct airplanes	0	1	2	3
7. Study the stars and changes in the universe	0	1	2	3
8. Test fertilizers and ways of growing crops	0	1	2	3
9. Analyze and forecast the financial conditions of the country	0	1	2	3
10. Develop chemical products in a laboratory	0	1	2	3
11. Experiment with cures for diseases	0	1	2	3
12. Search for and study artifacts from past civilizations	0	1	2	3
13. Study oceanic life	0	1	2	3
14. Work for NASA in aerospace experiments	0	1	2	3
15. Predict the weather for the National Weather Service	0	1	2	3
16. Fly commercial airplanes	0	1	2	3
17. Design technical computer programs	0	1	2	3
18. Test materials in a laboratory	0	1	2	3
19. Troubleshoot for electronics equipment repairs	0	1	2	3
20. Collect and classify rare stones	0	1	2	3
21. Diagnose illnesses and prescribe medication	0	1	2	3
22. Mix and dispense prescription medications at a drugstore	0	1	2	3
23. Complete medical tests in a lab or clinic	0	1	2	3
24. Perform surgery in a hospital	0	1	2	3
25. Teach science or mathematics in a high school	0	1	2	3
TOTALS				

Directions for totaling

Now go back and add together the numbers in each section. Each zero circled counts nothing. The ones are worth one point each; the twos are worth two points each; the threes are worth three points each. Write in the total score for each section on the line marked Total.

Compare the total figures in your Interest Indicator (Pages 20–25). What two groups received the highest number? (Group I: Body Workers; Group II: Data Detail; Group III: Persuaders; Group IV: The Service Workers; Group V: Creative Artists; Group VI: Investigators)

Which two groups did you select in the party exercise on pages 9–10? _____

The occupations that would interest you most are probably combinations of the groups you chose on the Interest Indicator and those selected in the party exercise.

Every job has characteristics of more than one occupational group; some parts of a job will resemble one occupational group, while other parts will resemble another. Thus in the Career Finder a two letter code has been given to each job title. For example, the code for teacher is SP, meaning that teachers most resemble the service workers group and also the persuader group, though somewhat less.

You can devise codes for occupations that might interest you. List some possible codes, combining your party and Interest Indicator choices. (For example, if you chose creative artists and service workers on the party exercise and service workers and persuaders on the Interest Indicator, possible codes are CS, PS, SC, SP, CP.) Write in your own codes here:

_____

_____

_____

Turn to the Career Finder on pages 67–104. Using the two-letter codes in the left column of the Career Finder, find up to five occupations that combine what you like to do and the kinds of people you like to be with. Write them below.

Skill Identification 5

Decide whether the following statements are *myths* or *facts*.

_____ I have no important skills and talents.

_____ Everyone is aware of his or her talents and skills.

_____ Most skills used in jobs are learned in school.

_____ Skills learned at home or on the street are rarely applicable to a job.

All of the above are common myths about skills. Most people wear blinders when they look at themselves. The fact is that skills learned not only in school but also in personal life are applicable to many jobs. In one survey of top managers, 51 percent rated an ability to get along with people as the most important skill they look for when hiring employees. This exercise is intended to open your eyes to the skills you have acquired in your life. It will help you to recognize your innermost talents.

In the diagonal blanks at the top of the chart on page 29, fill in ten accomplishments, jobs, or roles you have had. Emphasize parts of your life that you feel good about, regardless of whether they were formally recognized. The examples may be achievements like "I starred in the school play," "I learned to sew a tailored suit," "I tuned an automobile," or "I taught my little niece to tie her shoes." The examples could be paid jobs—babysitting, lawn care, or waiting on tables in a restaurant. Examples of different roles are student, worker, friend, housekeeper. Try to select examples, large or small, of things you have enjoyed doing and you feel good about. Think of some examples of the *best* you have ever done—the best personal relationship you ever had, the best paper you ever wrote.

Then read the list of skills and mark an X next to each skill you performed while completing your accomplishments. Put an O if you enjoyed performing that skill.

The example is filled out to describe the skills used by a girl working at a fast food franchise. She puts together customer's orders, so there is an X before "assemble." She sometimes sets up the milkshake machine and enjoys doing it. Thus there is an O before "operates tools." Reading, writing, and remembering are all a part of waiting on customers, so those skills are checked too. She has little opportunity to express herself in the work itself, so no items are marked under "freedom to use own ideas." Communicating with people, managing money, calculating figures, working rapidly with numbers, and collecting money are all a part of waiting on people and being a wage earner, so these skills, too, are marked.

Skill Chart

List 10 work, volunteer, school, or leisure experiences here:

Because I did this . . . .

I have this skill:

	example	1	2	3	4	5	6	7	8	9	10	Name of skill	Sample experience
	Work at McDonalds preparing food, waiting on customers				Sample							WORK WITH THINGS—SEE PHYSICAL RESULTS FROM WORK	
	X											Assemble	models
												Build	carpentry
												Install	appliances
	O											Operate tools	sewing machine, drill
												Shape	clay sculpture
												Type	
												Play musical instrument	
												Sew	

(continued)

Skill Identification   29

											Cut	fabric
											Photograph	snapshots, videotape
											Paint	artwork
											Draw	
X											Wash	cars, clothing
											Feed	babies, elderly
											Press	ironing
											Repair	cars, toys
											Drive	vehicles

WORK WITH IDEAS—USE INTELLECT

X											Read	instructions
X											Write	letters, orders
X											Instruct	
											Edit	rewrite
X											Remember	instructions, names
											Report	
											Translate	foreign language
											Speak	before groups

Skill Identification 31

	Summarize	club minutes
	Describe	writing letters
	Interview	

WORK WITH PEOPLE—ASSIST THEM IN HELPING RELATIONSHIP

	Assist	disabled person
x	Be sensitive to emotions	during disagreement
	Listen/understand	
x	Establish rapport	with new acquaintance
	Encourage	
	Raise other's self concept	
	Heal	physical wounds
	Advise	
	Draw out people	someone who is shy
	Reconcile	bring people together
x	Serve	take care of physical needs

WORK WITH PEOPLE USING PLEASING PERSONALITY

x	Initiate relationship	with stranger at school
	Organize	in a club

(continued)

32 *How to Choose the Right Career*

Direct others	officer in a club
Manage	direct other's work
Instruct	explanations
Converse	carry on lively conversations
Entertain	parties, make people laugh

WORK REQUIRING SELF EXPRESSION—FREEDOM TO USE OWN IDEAS

Imagine	think of new ways to do things
Invent, compose	stories, songs
Improvise, adapt	use equipment for purpose other than it was intended
Conceive	think of new ways to do things
Design	handicrafts
Create symbols or images	filmmaking, artwork
Combine colors	interior design, fashion coordination
Convey emotions and ideas	acting, public speaking, dancing
Use words imaginatively	creative writing

WORK AS PART OF A TEAM

Share credit, appreciation	
Cooperate	

Skill Identification 33

Consult											
Help											x
Take instructions											x

WORK DEMANDING PHYSICAL STAMINA

Perform	act on stage										
Carry, lift											
Deliver											
Operate machines	snowblower, lawn mower										x
Paint	walls										
Use muscular coordination	gymnastics, swimming										
Use eye-hand coordination	video games										
Care for animals	groom										

WORK WITH DETAILS

Inventory, count	store, kitchen										
Calculate, compute	bankbook										

(continued)

34 *How to Choose the Right Career*

	Manage money	Budget	Remember numbers	Work rapidly with numbers	Estimate	Collect	Measure	Use statistics	Classify	Remember facts	Follow detailed instructions	Classify	Record	File	Retrieve	Transcribe
tax records																
allocating expenses																
phone numbers																
calculate in head																
total future charges																
cashier																
cooking																
conduct survey																
filing																
objective tests																
assemble bike																
shorthand																
	o			o	x											

Skill Identification **35**

WORK WITH PEOPLE, MOTIVATING AND PERSUADING THEM

Organize, recruit, enlist	mobilize people to action
Raise funds	collect for charity
Stimulate	give rousing speech
Sell, negotiate	garage sale
Persuade	debate, editorials
Lead, direct others	cheerleading, team captain
Supervise	child care
Motivate	persuade someone to change
Arbitrate	settle family argument
Divert	draw people's attention from one thing to another

Recognizing your skills is important in deciding what career you would like to try. Look back over the skill chart and decide which three areas you are strongest in. Put a check before each skill you possess.

		Career Finder Number
_____	Work physically with things	7
_____	Work with ideas	8
_____	Work with people—helping them	9
_____	Work with people—using pleasing personality	10
_____	Work requiring self-expression	12
_____	Work as part of a team	13
_____	Work demanding physical stamina	21
_____	Work with details and data	22
_____	Work motivating and persuading people	24

Relating Your Skills to Desirable Careers

The nine skill titles used in the preceding chart are the same as the job characteristics listed in the Career Finder pages 67–104. Use the Career Finder or your imagination and knowledge of the outside world to detect jobs which would use skills you now have. For example, if your strongest job skills are 7, 13, and 22, you might consider being a lithographer.

Skill/Career Relationship

List your top three skills, and try to think of an attractive career option that uses these skills. Write down the name of the career whether or not you have all the skills needed for it now.

Skill   *Attractive career which uses skill*

1. _____   1. _____

2. _____   2. _____

3. _____   3. _____

What skills do you need to develop for each career you find appealing?

Appealing career   *Skill to develop*

1. _____   1. _____

2. _____   2. _____

3. _____   3. _____

How can the missing skills be acquired?

Missing skills   *Way to acquire missing skills*

1. _____   1. _____

2. _____   2. _____

3. _____   3. _____

Now delve deeper into your memory bank and try to identify other unique experiences that might give you a special background that others have not had. Think of careers experienced by members of your family or friends from which you have learned a great deal, or perhaps you have been part of special projects that other people have not experienced. Think of unusual people you have known, books that have taught you special things. Beside each experience that you list, try to define the skill that you feel you have obtained as a result of that experience.

Experience	*Skills*
(Sample)	
Daughter of writer/publisher	Know what is involved in getting something into print.
Owner and caretaker of four pets	Good understanding of animal care
Avid sports fan	Know rules for many games
Read many mysteries	Know how crimes are solved

How to Choose the Right Career

Experience	Skills
_____	_____
_____	_____
_____	_____
_____	_____
_____	_____
_____	_____
_____	_____
_____	_____
_____	_____
_____	_____
_____	_____
_____	_____
_____	_____
_____	_____
_____	_____

Now use the following Career Investigation Sheet to investigate another career that interests you. List the career, and think it over as you write, noting what is required and whether you can accept the requirements and conditions of the job.

Career Investigation Sheet

Career that interests you _____

	Won't Accept	Unsure	Will Accept

Training or education requirements:

_____

_____

_____

Job description: (What would you do all day?)

_____

_____

_____

Work environment: (office/factory, indoor/outdoor)

_____

_____

_____

Earning potential: (How much will I start earning? How much will I eventually make?)

_____

_____

_____

Employment outlook: (Will there be jobs after I complete the necessary education?)

_____

_____

_____

Job Characteristics 6

Think about the following questions:

- How much education would you like your career to require?
- Where do you want to work?
- Do you want to work with people, information, or things?
- How much freedom of self-expression do you require?
- Do you want to work alone or as part of a team?
- Do you want to supervise others, or do you want them to supervise you?
- How much responsibility do you want?
- How do you feel about working with details?

- How do you feel about performing the same task over and over?

Knowing the answers to some of these questions can help you find a satisfying career. Begin the process by deciding the importance of the following job factors. Circle the factors that are important to you.

JOB ENVIRONMENT
Pleasant surroundings
Private working space
Piped-in music
Exercise facilities
Company cafeteria
Windows or view
Nonsmoking environment
Work primarily outdoors
Travel frequently

COMPENSATION
Fair salary
Commission on sales
Royalty
Bonuses
Frequent salary review
Health insurance
Dental insurance
Company car
Tuition reimbursements
Predictable promotions
Chance to advance rapidly

TIME
Set work schedule
Flexible work schedule
Extensive vacations
Overtime
No overtime

Work to take home
Work weekends
Night work
Regular lunch hours
Regular routine
Paid holidays
Summers free

PEOPLE CONTACT
Work alone
Supervise others
Work independently
Work closely supervised
Work in large organization
Work in small business

SCHOOLING REQUIRED
High school
Apprenticeship
Technical school
Associate's degree
Bachelor's degree
Master's degree
Doctorate

Now look back over your list of wants and compose an advertisement you could write describing the characteristics of the job you want: _____

Job Characteristics **43**

Think over the characteristics you have listed on the previous page and consider what jobs have many or even all of these characteristics. List the jobs below, and also jot down any thoughts you have about the limitations the jobs might pose. Would you need to know more about requirements? Would you need additional training? Would you need to move to a different part of the country? Write down your thoughts, after each job name, and keep your list for further reference as you consider your career possibilities.

Job: _____

_____

_____

_____

_____

_____

Job: _____

_____

_____

_____

_____

_____

Job: _____

_____

_____

_____

_____

_____

Rewards and Satisfactions 7

Each job differs in what you do all day: the work itself, the people you work with, and the kinds of rewards you receive. The rewards are not just money, but the kind of feeling you get from doing the job.

What is rewarding to one person may be unimportant to another. Some people want to be rich. Some want to help others. Some want to create beautiful art. The secret is to define the rewards that are important to you, because you will never be motivated until you find an activity that is meaningful to you.

Everyone needs the feeling that what they are doing is worthwhile. The more people understand the value of their work, the more motivated they will be to do it.

REWARDS AND SATISFACTIONS

On the next pages are six different job titles. Explain why you think someone would enjoy each job—what the rewards of the work are.

Professional Football Player

Rewards: _____

_____
_____
_____
_____
_____
_____
_____
_____

Secretary

Rewards: _____

_____
_____
_____
_____
_____
_____
_____
_____

Politician

Rewards:

Veterinarian

Rewards:

Artist

Rewards:_____

_____

_____

_____

_____

_____

_____

_____

Scientist

Rewards:_____

_____

_____

_____

_____

_____

_____

_____

Different people find rewards and motivation from different things. For some, satisfaction comes from a sense of achievement at seeing the work that is completed. These people are often called the **Body Workers**. They enjoy seeing the real, concrete results of their work. Others feel good at helping an organization run smoothly, being part of an efficient business. The people who are motivated by this kind of reward are often the **Data Detail** people. The **Persuaders** enjoy seeing things happen. They have a sense of achievement from mobilizing people and ideas. Many persuaders are paid in proportion to their achievements, so money is often a payoff for being a successful persuader. For the **Service Workers**, the joy of helping people is usually the greatest reward. The thrill of the creative process, of being involved in the conception and actualization of an idea, is the greatest reward of the **Creative Artists**. The **Investigators** enjoy analyzing things—seeing how they work.

The following list includes some of the many different rewards of working. Select the five rewards that you would like most to be part of your career, putting a check before each one.

_____ Have responsibilities that change frequently

_____ Work in situations with little room for error

_____ Have close working relationships with others

_____ Do projects alone, without much contact with others

_____ Pit abilities against others with clear win-lose results

_____ Work under pressure

_____ Control the work or destiny of others

_____ Search for knowledge or truth

_____ Create new programs without following a previous format

_____ Study and appreciate beauty

_____ Have a predictable work routine

_____ Work without much direction from others

_____ Work on own time schedule

_____ Other rewards _____

Now try to think of three careers which would provide all or most of the rewards you desire.

1. _____

2. _____

3. _____

Use career references, the Career Finder in this book, the want ad lists in the newspaper, or any other sources to give you ideas of possibilities. Consider the rewards and satisfactions of each possibility carefully.

Getting Field Experience 8

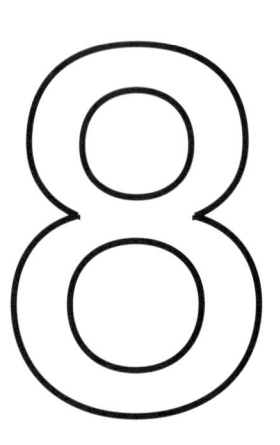

Most career fields have volunteer or part-time opportunities available where a young person can gain experience that will help in making an informed career choice. All that is needed is a willingness to give your time on a regular, scheduled basis.

"I majored in special education in college, did my student teaching in my senior year, and discovered that it wasn't for me. I sure wasted a lot of time and money, majoring in something I don't want to do."

—Sue, a 22-year-old woman, now cleans airplanes for an airline.

"I'm a trainee in a computer programming department but I don't enjoy working in an office. I can't stand being cooped up all the time.

It's a good job, but not for me. Trouble is, I can't afford to give up the salary while I check out things I'd like to do better."

—Dan, a 27-year-old man, working in a corporate programming department.

If Sue had volunteered or worked part time as a teacher's aide, camp counselor, or tutor, she might have had a better understanding of the rewards and aggravations of working with children. If Dan had volunteered or worked part time at office work, he might have learned that he was better suited to a less confining job.

Have you learned that there are some jobs that you definitely do not want? Work environments that you would not like? Certain types of work that are not for you? Jot down these items on the lines below.

_____

_____

_____

_____

_____

Getting Experience through Volunteer and Part-Time Work
Places to work as a body worker

Small Machine Repair. If you want to learn about repairing broken typewriters, adding machines, and copying equipment, contact your local Volunteer Action Center or a small-business owner. Many charitable organizations repair donated equipment and can use people who are willing to learn to do careful work, and many small businesses can use part-time workers.

Fire Fighting. Call your local fire department and ask for suggestions for increasing your understanding of careers in the fire department. A volunteer fire department may offer a volunteer training program if you live in a rural area.

Conservation and Forestry. The Isaac Walton League, Sierra Club, and Audubon Society publish helpful information and provide opportunities for gaining experience. Museums of natural science, botanic gardens, and zoos all offer work with plants and animals. It could be worth doing menial work to be near experts in the field. If you become knowledgeable, you might become a tour guide, explain displays to visiting groups, or be part of a conservation crew that will give you valuable experience.

Agriculture. Future Farmers of America and 4-H Clubs use volunteers to help lead activities. Some residential care facilities, such as halfway houses, encourage residents to have gardens and need volunteers to help with the programs. Summer work may be available on farms as well.

Landscape Architecture. Public gardens and park districts often use volunteers who can learn first-hand about specific needs of plants, shrubs, and trees for shade, sun, water, fertilizer, and special maintenance. In addition, much of the work of commercial landscape architects is done in spring and summer. Call early to line up a summer job.

Cooking or Baking. Local Meals-on-Wheels programs deliver hot meals to disabled people. Volunteers are often used in the kitchen where the demands of volume cooking can be observed first-hand. Part-time jobs for evenings or weekends in bakeries, restaurant kitchens, pizza shops, or other carryout food restaurants are useful.

Upholstery and Furniture Repair. Many organizations need help in repairing furniture. Contact your local Volunteer Action Center for information. Check in the Yellow Pages of the telephone directory to locate businesses where you may be able to get part-time work and training.

Places to work as an investigator

History. Some libraries employ students to interview local residents as part of oral history projects. Museums likewise welcome volunteers. Historical societies also provide opportunities for research and library aides.

Veterinary Medicine. Convince a local veterinarian that you could be helpful cleaning cages, feeding animals, sorting medicines, and preparing examining rooms, and you will have a good opportunity to see the day-to-day work of animal health care. Animal shelters and the Humane Society also welcome volunteers.

Optometry. The Society for the Prevention of Blindness concerns itself with sight-saving projects. Volunteers help screen preschoolers for vision problems and tutors and aides work in training centers for the blind.

Places to work as a creative artist

Architecture. Few volunteer responsibilities are available for high school students, but fifth-year architectural graduate students can work as paraprofessionals in Community Design Centers (CDC), many sponsored by the American Institute of Architects. These centers provide services to people who cannot afford to employ an architect for one small project, such as an addition to a private home. Related industries such as real estate, construction, or landmark preservation groups may provide part-time work, either paid or volunteer.

Art. Day care centers, day camps, Y's, and community centers often need volunteer teachers to work with children in the arts. Hundreds of organizations sponsor boutiques or bazaars where individual creations can be exhibited and sold. Communicating a willingness to do any task at an art museum (filing, gift shop sales, dusting artifacts) offers contact with the work of other artists. A brief course in keyline and pasteup will provide students with a skill for part-time work for commercial artists and designers.

Interior Design. Part-time work for a furniture store or a wholesale furniture showroom will allow you to observe how current styles are being used. It will also allow you to find out who the best interior designers are and what their work is like. With experience in the furniture showrooms, you may next be able to land a part-time job as an interior designer's helper.

Writing. To practice writing, volunteer to help with some organization's newsletter. Any volunteer experience that allows you to observe how writers work for a living will help you to make a more realistic career choice.

Fashion. Department stores provide opportunities to learn about fashion trends and design. Helping a buyer or window dresser, or doing part-time sales clerking in a good store will give you useful information.

Advertising and Public Relations. Many community organizations need to be better known within a community. Emergency care agencies and hotlines should be known to people in the area they serve; senior citizens should be aware of the services available to them in their communities. Volunteer to type press releases and contact the local press about activities that should be publicized.

Some large hospitals offer volunteers the opportunity to work with public relations professionals on a variety of projects such as newsletters, press releases, photo arrangements, and fund raising. If you can stuff envelopes, type, or file, try the commercial agencies for a part-time or temporary job.

Performing Arts. Recordings for the Blind and The Braille Institute offer volunteer opportunities for performers to make records of recent books, plays, songs, and magazine articles.

Many hospitals and convalescent homes have an unending stream of entertainers at Christmas but could use some diversion the rest of the year. Professional theaters, opera houses, and regional theaters have apprenticeship programs in which the pay is low, and the waiting list is usually long. The Actors Equity office in any large city will be able to give you names and addresses of the theaters in your area.

You should apply a year ahead of time. Get your name on the list, and keep calling and dropping by to remind them of your application until you get the job.

Places to work as a service worker

Counseling and Psychology. Hotlines and telephone crisis services for teenagers employ teenagers as well as adults. Their training courses can be valuable in learning how to help people in crisis situations. Halfway houses and social clubs for former mental patients offer controlled situations ideal for the beginning volunteer.

Teaching. Working with children in educational or recreation programs sponsored by community, civic, and religious groups will give you experience with normal children.

Organizations that help handicapped children also offer experience in rehabilitative education. Many public and private schools welcome teacher's aides and tutors on a regular basis. Day care centers may be a source of part-time work.

Personnel. Youth employment services available in some communities try to place students in full- or part-time jobs. Volunteers interview students, advise them on how to go about a job interview, and contact possible employers. If there is no youth employment service in your area, you may be able to start one at a nearby school with the help of a faculty advisor.

Library Science. Volunteers at hospitals are sometimes used to deliver books to patients, do storytelling for children, and assist in making displays, decorations, and posters for children's rooms. Part-time work may be available in your school library or a private or public library in the community.

Home Economics. The majority of home economists teach, so it would be wise to get some teaching experience. The Girl Scouts, Camp Fire Girls, and 4-H Clubs have cooking, nutrition, and clothing activities, and they welcome willing volunteers. Many halfway houses teach domestic skills, and visiting nurse programs sometimes use volunteers to instruct people on maintaining their homes, cooking, and nutrition.

Health Services. Large hospitals often have a formal volunteer program which gives a wide range of experience. Some volunteers work in emergency and physical therapy departments, and some gain high school credit in work/study arrangements. Convalescent hospitals offer the opportunity to work with senior citizens and recuperating patients.

Public Contact Work. Hospitals provide opportunities to volunteers in admitting, and gift shops. Some volunteers have contact with patients while passing mail and delivering menus. Religious and public service organizations often have volunteer programs in hospitals. Choose a hospital you'd like to work in, and talk with the volunteer coordinator or the personnel department.

Places to work as a persuader

Legal Professions. The Legal Aid Society and some public defender staffs welcome volunteers or part-time workers to run errands, do clerical work, and answer telephones. Work as a part-time secretary in a law office, a courthouse, or Bar Association office will provide exposure to legal work.

Politics. Many modern presidents began their careers in local politics. A great deal can be learned about campaigning by working door-to-door, phoning voters, stuffing envelopes, and passing flyers. Local politicians and school board and park district representatives often need help. The League of Women Voters keeps tabs on local government and operates an effective information service about government structures, representatives and issues. Membership is open to men and women over age 18. All political parties welcome volunteers; so do all candidates for office. Some paid positions are sometimes also available.

Sales. Part-time or summer work as a salesperson will allow you to try your hand at convincing others of the need to buy—whether you are selling candy, brushes, or real estate, you will find out if you can sell.

Places to work in the data detail

Banking. Many organizations have credit unions. Loans are made to depositors, interest is charged, and profit sharing is paid to shareholders. Information on starting a credit union can be obtained from the National Credit Union Administration, Washington, D.C. 02456. A part-time job in a bank will give you a chance to observe various kinds of workers in their jobs.

Accounting. Every organization that collects dues and receives contributions needs a treasurer. Serving as a volunteer treasurer will allow you to practice the basics. You will need some bookkeeping and accounting courses to get part-time accounting work.

Travel Industry. The Traveler's Aid Society offers people the opportunity to learn some of the problems facing travelers. The International Student Service is an organization that greets visiting students from other countries who want to sightsee before reaching their place of schooling. Contact travel agents in your community for part-time work and to discuss training needs.

Clerical Work. Virtually every public service organization needs clerical assistance. The United Fund, consumer bureaus, public health offices, and free clinics are but a few of the places that would welcome clerical help.

58 *How to Choose the Right Career*

Field Experience Observation Sheet

Select three organizations that could use volunteer or part-time help you can provide. Write the names, addresses, and phone numbers on the sheet below. Phone them and ask to speak with the person in charge of the human resources or personnel department. Explain what you would like to do, and ask if work is available. If it is not, ask the person to give you suggestions about other organizations to call, or other information you should have.

Name: _____

Address: _____

Contact: _____

Observations: _____

_____

Name: _____

Address: _____

Contact: _____

Observations: _____

_____

Name: _____

Address: _____

Contact: _____

Observations: _____

_____

Name: _____

Address: _____

Contact: _____

Observations: _____

_____

The Advice Interview   9

Reading about an occupation seldom gives someone enough motivation to choose a career. The real interest develops from individual experience, from personal encouragement, and talking with people who are enthusiastic about their work. It is important to find and talk with people who work in fields that interest you.

Use family members, friends, and other contacts for introductions to people working in specific occupations. Explain that you are using a career program workbook to search out a career and that you want to interview people working in fields that you find attractive. Ask people to meet with you or at least to answer questions over the telephone. If the first people you ask refuse, keep trying. There are many people who enjoy talking about their jobs or helping others find direction.

Here are some questions worth asking:

- How did you happen to choose this occupation?
- What do you like best about it?
- What do you like least?
- What kind of people tend to do well in this career?
- Do you do the same thing all day long, or is there variety?
- Can you think of some particular event on your job that made you feel good? What was it?
- What kinds of things happen on the job to make you angry or sad?
- What are the opportunities for the future?
- What kinds of problems does this industry have? Labor? Costs?
- What do you see as the purposes, goals, and values of your employer?
- What qualifications are needed to do the job? What training?
- Can you recommend other people for me to talk to?
- Who might hire me for an entry-level job in this area once I get the qualifications?

Possible Interviews

List names of people you could interview about jobs and careers.

Name	Position	Special notes

Whose job would you like most to have? Why? _____

_____

_____

_____

_____

_____

What do you need to do to get that job? _____

_____

_____

_____

_____

_____

Research a Career 10

One of the greatest and most common career mistakes is not choosing a career because you are unaware that it exists. Any library contains many tools for investigation that can be used to uncover interesting career possibilities.

Excellent reference books   *Dictionary of Occupational Titles.* As big as a telephone book from a major city, the D.O.T. is a great source of occupational information. It lists over 20,000 job titles and describes them by physical demands, working conditions, interest, educational requirements, and vocational preparation. A code number identifies workers' involvement with information, people, and things.

Occupational Outlook Handbook. Less technical to use than the D.O.T., this book describes the employment outlook, work, required training, earnings, and working conditions for several hundred occupations.

Encyclopedia of Career and Vocational Guidance. This source provides specific information on salaries and also lists educational requirements, advancement possibilities, and specific demands for over 650 occupations.

Occupational Guidance. This easy-to-read eight-volume set describes the job; earnings; history; working conditions; hours; requirements, temperament, and abilities needed; education; attractive and unattractive features; and suggested high school courses. It even gives questions to test your interest in specific fields.

The card catalog

Check the computer or card catalog. Look under individual occupations that interest you to locate books that you may take home. For instance, look under *A* for aviation, *O* for office work.

The vertical file

Many libraries store excellent pamphlets on individual careers under *C* in the vertical files. You may have to ask the librarian to get materials from the vertical files.

Professional journals and directories

Almost every career field has its own magazine or a professional journal which gives updates on the special situations facing people in that occupation. Articles often contain names of people to contact directly about employment. Many such journals also list job openings.

Library reference departments also have directories that list employers in specific industries. The largest directories are as follows:

Dun and Bradstreet Million Dollar Directories. (3 volumes: Volume 1 lists firms with net worth over $1.2 million; Volume 2, firms with net worth between $900 thousand and $1.2 million; Volume 3, firms with net worth between $500 and $900 thousand. Gives locations, products, executives' names, number of employees.): Dun and Bradstreet, 99 Church Street, New York, New York 10004.

Standard & Poor's Register of Corporations, Directors, and Executives. (400,000 key executives in 38,000 leading companies cross-referenced by product and company location. Includes home addresses of executives plus title and duties): Standard & Poor's Corporation, 25 Broadway, New York, New York 10004.

The Composite Picture 11

Crime witnesses frequently work with police artists in drafting composite pictures of suspects. At this point you can assemble all the clues from your career search and draw a composite picture of the career that would make you happy. Go back over the exercises in this book and summarize what you have learned about the job that will make you happiest.

- Your dream job
- Strongest skills
- Rewards that will make you happy
- Job characteristics you don't want
- Job characteristics you do want
- Kinds of co-workers you want
- Important, ultimate life goals
- Prime job possibilities so far

Use the following worksheet to write out all your thoughts on these subjects. Remember, too, that all of these thoughts will change during your lifetime to some degree; this is your Job Needs Profile for right now, and the foreseeable future—you'll want to assess your needs and preferences again, later on, perhaps many times.

Job Needs Profile

_____
_____
_____
_____
_____
_____
_____
_____
_____
_____
_____
_____
_____
_____
_____
_____
_____
_____
_____

The Career Finder 12

The Career Finder on the following pages gives you an extensive checklist of information about many kinds of jobs and their characteristics. Each job listing is coded for the type of job group with a two-letter code. This is the same letter code you have used in your previous worksheets and activities. Footnotes—indicated by numbers 1–8 and symbols T, +, A, *, **— are explained after the last page of the Career Finder, page 104.

Each job listing is followed by numbered columns which provide information about the job's requirements or characteristics. This information includes the estimated number of workers in the field at present, the projected openings each year, and the employment picture for the future.

Directions: Look back at the work you did in Chapter 5 on pages 27–36. Using the Career Finder numbers that you identified at the top of page 36, select your strongest job skill columns in the Career Finder Chart pages 70–104. You may want to mark these columns with a colored highlighter pen through the whole chart, to make it easy to identify jobs that include your strongest skills.

25 Common Job Skills and Characteristics

These 25 job skills and characteristics are keyed to the Career Finder on the following pages. An *X* appears in the numbered column on the Career Finder whenever the corresponding skill or characteristic is related to the specific job.

1. High school diploma generally required.
2. Technical school or apprenticeship. Some form of nondegree post–high school training required.
3. Junior college degree. Requires Associate in Arts degree.
4. College degree. Requires at least a bachelor's degree.
5. Jobs widely scattered. Jobs are located in most areas of the United States.
6. Jobs concentrated in one or a few geographical locations.
7. Work with things. Jobs generally require manual skills.
8. Work with ideas. Use one's intellect to solve problems.
9. Help people. Assist people in a helping relationship.
10. Work with people. Job generally requires pleasing personality and ability to get along with others.
11. Able to see physical results of work. Work produces a tangible product.
12. Opportunity for self-expression. Freedom to use one's own ideas.
13. Work as part of a team. Interact with fellow employees in performing work.
14. Work independently. Requires self-discipline and ability to organize.
15. Work is closely supervised. Job performance and work standards controlled.
16. Direct activities of others. Work entails supervisory responsibilities.
17. Generally confined to work area. Physically located at one work setting.
18. Overtime or shift work required. Work hours other than normal daytime shifts.
19. Outdoors. Exposed to weather or is subjected to temperature extremes.
20. High level of responsibility. Requires making key decisions involving property, finances, or human safety and welfare.
21. Requires physical stamina. Must be in physical condition for continued lifting, standing, and walking.
22. Work with details. Work with technical data, numbers, or written materials on a continuous basis.
23. Repetitious work. Perform the same task on a continuous basis.
24. Motivate others. Must be able to influence others.
25. Competitive. Compete with other people on the job.

70 *How to Choose the Right Career*

Column headers (TYPE OF WORK AND CO-WORKERS):
1. High School diploma
2. Technical school or apprenticeship
3. Junior college
4. College degree
5. Jobs widely scattered
6. Jobs concentrated in locations
7. Work with things
8. Work with ideas
9. Help people
10. Work with people
11. Able to see physical results of work
12. Opportunity for self-expression
13. Work as part of a team
14. Work independently
15. Work closely supervised
16. Direct activity of others
17. Generally confined to work area
18. Overtime or shift work required
19. Outdoors
20. High level of responsibility
21. Requires physical stamina
22. Work with detail
23. Repetitious work
24. Motivate others
25. Competitive

FOUNDRY OCCUPATIONS

	Occupation	1	2	3	4	5	6	7	8	9	10	11	12	13	14	15	16	17	18	19	20	21	22	23	24	25	Est. Emp. 1990	Range of Change (hundreds) 1990-2000	Employment Prospects
BI**	Patternmakers	X	A					X				X		X		X		X			X		X				3,000	6 to 9	Employment expected to grow more slowly than average. Use of durable metal patterns will offset increases in foundry productions.
BI	Molders*		A					X			X	X		X		X		X			X		X				22,000	9 to 20	Below average.
BI	Coremakers		A					X			X	X		X		X	X	X					X	X			6,200	6 to 9	Employment expected to increase more slowly than average as growing use of machine coremaking limits the need for additional workers.

MACHINING OCCUPATIONS

	Occupation	1	2	3	4	5	6	7	8	9	10	11	12	13	14	15	16	17	18	19	20	21	22	23	24	25	Est. Emp. 1990	Range of Change (hundreds) 1990-2000	Employment Prospects
BI	All-around machinists*		A					X				X		X		X		X			X		X	X			397,000	18 to 21	Employment expected to increase slower than average.
BI	Instrument makers*	X	A				X	X				X		X		X	X	X			X		X	X			43,000	18 to 33	Average. Laborsaving innovations may limit growth.
BI	Machine tool operators*—metal and plastic		X					X				X		X		X		X			X		X	X			1,405,000	18 to 21	Few new jobs expected.
BI	Setup Workers*	X	A				X	X				X		X		X		X			X		X	X			93,000	21 to 30	Average, however advances in toolmaking may limit growth.

The Career Finder

Column headers (TYPE OF WORK AND CO-WORKERS)

1. High School diploma
2. Technical school or apprenticeship
3. Junior college
4. College degree
5. Jobs widely scattered
6. Jobs concentrated in locations
7. Work with things
8. Work with ideas
9. Help people
10. Work with people
11. Able to see physical results of work
12. Opportunity for self-expression
13. Work as part of a team
14. Work independently
15. Work closely supervised
16. Direct activity of others
17. Generally confined to work area
18. Overtime or shift work required
19. Outdoors
20. High level of responsibility
21. Requires physical stamina
22. Work with detail
23. Repetitious work
24. Motivate others
25. Competitive

MACHINING OCCUPATIONS

Code	Occupation	1	2	3	4	5	6	7	8	9	10	11	12	13	14	15	16	17	18	19	20	21	22	23	24	25	Estimated Employment – 1990	Range of possible change 1990–2000	Employment Prospects
BI	Tool-and-die makers*				A		X	X				X			X			X	X				X X				152,000	8 to 24	Employment expected to grow more slowly than average as advances in toolmaking processes limit growth. Because of a shortage of experienced workers, excellent job opportunities expected.

PRINTING OCCUPATIONS

Code	Occupation	1	2	3	4	5	6	7	8	9	10	11	12	13	14	15	16	17	18	19	20	21	22	23	24	25	Estimated Employment – 1990	Range of possible change 1990–2000	Employment Prospects
BC	Compositors	X	A				X	X						X		X		X	X				X X				128,000	−2 to 10	Declining due to high-speed phototypesetting and typesetting computers. Best prospects for graduates of professional printing technology courses.
BC	Lithographers	X	A				X	X						X		X		X	X				X X				44,000	29 to 33	Employment expected to be slower than average. Best job prospects for graduates of postsecondary school programs in printing technology.
BD	Photoengravers	X	A				X	X				X		X		X		X	X				X X				23,000	−5 to −3	Declining because of switch from letterpress to offset printing.
BD	Electrotypers and stereotypers	X	A				X	X				X		X		X		X	X				X X				1,800	−19 to −21	Declining due to greater use of offset printing and other laborsaving equipment.
BI	Printing press operators and assistants*	X	A				X	X						X		X			X			X	X X				239,000	9 to 17	Slowing as faster and more efficient presses limit growth.

72 *How to Choose the Right Career*

OCCUPATION		1	2	3	4	5	6	7	8	9	10	11	12	13	14	15	16	17	18	19	20	21	22	23	24	25	ESTIMATED EMPLOYMENT – 1990	RANGE OF POSSIBLE CHANGE IN EMPLOYMENT (HUNDREDS) 1990-2000	EMPLOYMENT PROSPECTS

Column headings (1–25): Competitive; Motivate others; Repetitious work; Work with detail; Requires physical stamina; High level of responsibility; Outdoors; Overtime or shift work required; Generally confined to work area; Direct activity of others; Work closely supervised; Work independently; Work as part of a team; Opportunity for self-expression; Able to see physical results of work; Work with people; Help people; Work with ideas; Work with things; Jobs concentrated in locations; Jobs widely scattered; College degree; Junior college; Technical school or apprenticeship; High School diploma

PRINTING OCCUPATIONS

	Occupation	1	2	3	4	5	6	7	8	9	10	11	12	13	14	15	16	17	18	19	20	21	22	23	24	25	Est. Empl. 1990	Range 1990-2000	Prospects
BC	Bookbinders and binder workers*	X	A			X	X	X	X			X						X						X	X		73,000	3 to 6	Average rate of growth.

OTHER INDUSTRIAL PRODUCTION AND RELATED OCCUPATIONS

	Occupation	1	2	3	4	5	6	7	8	9	10	11	12	13	14	15	16	17	18	19	20	21	22	23	24	25	Est. Empl. 1990	Range 1990-2000	Prospects
BD	Assemblers		X	X		X	X							X	X	X		X						X	X		1,670,000	19 to 21	Average growth due to demand for consumer products and industrial equipment. Economic changes and national defense spending often affect job opportunities.
BD	Automobile painters*		X			X	X	X				X			X	X		X	X					X			40,000	21 to 26	Employment expected to increase slower than average.
PB	Blue-collar workers supervisors	X	(1)	(1)	(1)					X				X		X	X	X	X		X						1,250,000	16 to 21	Employment expected to increase about as fast as average. Large part of increase in nonmanufacturing industries.

CLERICAL OCCUPATIONS

	Occupation	1	2	3	4	5	6	7	8	9	10	11	12	13	14	15	16	17	18	19	20	21	22	23	24	25	Est. Empl. 1990	Range 1990-2000	Prospects
DI	Bookkeepers and accounting clerks	X			X		X							X	X	X		X					X	X	X		2,252,000	19 to 21	Increasing use of bookkeeping machines and electronic computers will limit growth. Due to high replacement needs, job opportunities are still expected to be numerous.
DI	Cashiers				X					X				X	X	X		X					X	X	X		2,310,000	24 to 28	Average growth expected due to rising retail trade.

TYPE OF WORK AND CO-WORKERS

The Career Finder

CLERICAL OCCUPATIONS

	OCCUPATION	Jobs widely scattered (1)	Jobs concentrated in locations (2)	Work with things (3)	Work with ideas (4)	Help people (5)	Work with people (6)	Able to see physical results of work (7)	Opportunity for self-expression (8)	Work as part of a team (9)	Work independently (10)	Work closely supervised (11)	Direct activity of others (12)	Generally confined to work area (13)	Overtime or shift work required (14)	Outdoors (15)	High level of responsibility (16)	Requires physical stamina (17)	Work with detail (18)	Repetitious work (19)	Motivate others (20)	Competitive (21)	High School diploma (22)	Technical school or apprenticeship (23)	Junior college (24)	College degree (25)	ESTIMATED EMPLOYMENT – 1990	RANGE OF POSSIBLE CHANGE IN EMPLOYMENT (HUNDREDS) 1990-2000	EMPLOYMENT PROSPECTS
DP	Hotel front office clerks	X					X			X	X				X			X	X				X				113,000	19 to 21	Employment expected to grow faster than average. The use of computerized reservation systems may limit growth.
DB	Typists	X					X	X				X			X	X		X	X	X			X				1,100,000	18 to 25	Employment expected to grow as fast as average as business expansion increases the amount of paperwork. Replacement needs will remain high. Demand particularly strong for typists who can handle a variety of office duties and operate word-processing equipment.
DB	Computer-operating personnel	X	X				X	X						X	X			X	X	X			X	X			312,000	19 to 20	Employment of console and peripheral equipment operators expected to rise faster than average as use of computers expands. Employment of keypunch operators expected to decline, however, due to more efficient direct data entry techniques.
ID	Programmers	X (1)	(1)				X		X					X	X		X	X					X				519,000	29 to 33	Employment expected to grow much faster than average as computer usage expands, particularly in accounting, business management, data-processing services, and research and development. Brightest prospects for college graduates with degree in computer science or related field.
PI	Systems analysts				X		X		X					X									X				235,000	46 to 60	Excellent prospects for graduates of computer-related curriculums.

74 *How to Choose the Right Career*

Column headers (TYPE OF WORK AND CO-WORKERS):
1. High School diploma
2. Technical school or apprenticeship
3. Junior college
4. College degree
5. Jobs widely scattered
6. Jobs concentrated in locations
7. Work with things
8. Work with ideas
9. Help people
10. Work with people
11. Able to see physical results of work
12. Opportunity for self-expression
13. Work as part of a team
14. Work independently
15. Work closely supervised
16. Direct activity of others
17. Generally confined to work area
18. Overtime or shift work required
19. Outdoors
20. High level of responsibility
21. Requires physical stamina
22. Work with detail
23. Repetitious work
24. Motivate others
25. Competitive

BANKING OCCUPATIONS

	Occupation	1	2	3	4	5	6	7	8	9	10	11	12	13	14	15	16	17	18	19	20	21	22	23	24	25	Est. Employment 1990	Range of change 1990–2000 (hundreds)	Employment Prospects
DI	Bank clerks	X				X					X	X						X			X		X	X			1,000,000	26 to 32	Employment expected to grow faster than average as banking services expand.
PD	Bank officers and managers	X			X	X								X		X	X				X		X	X	X		389,000	28 to 33	Employment expected to grow slower than average. Competition for managerial positions likely to stiffen.
DP	Bank tellers	X				X					X	X				X	X	X			X		X	X			522,000	26 to 29	Employment expected to grow faster than average as banks expand services. Opportunities for both full-time and part-time positions should be good.

INSURANCE OCCUPATIONS

	Occupation	1	2	3	4	5	6	7	8	9	10	11	12	13	14	15	16	17	18	19	20	21	22	23	24	25	Est. Employment 1990	Range of change 1990–2000 (hundreds)	Employment Prospects
ID	Actuaries				X	X			X						X		X	X			X		X	X			16,000	40 to 48	Employment expected to rise faster than average as insurance sales increase and insurance companies introduce new forms of insurance and reevaluate existing health and pension plans.
ID	Claim representatives	(1)	(1)		X		X				X	X			X				X				X				231,000	39 to 46	Employment expected to grow faster than average due to increasing insurance claims.
PI	Underwriters				X		X		X														X				103,000	22 to 29	Employment expected to grow as fast as average as insurance sales expand.

The Career Finder **75**

ADMINISTRATIVE AND RELATED OCCUPATIONS

	OCCUPATION	1	2	3	4	5	6	7	8	9	10	11	12	13	14	15	16	17	18	19	20	21	22	23	24	25	ESTIMATED EMPLOYMENT – 1990	RANGE OF POSSIBLE CHANGE IN EMPLOYMENT (HUNDREDS) 1990-2000	EMPLOYMENT PROSPECTS
PI	Lawyers	+	X						X	X			X		X				X		X				X	X	622,000	26 to 40	Keen competition likely for salaried positions. Best prospects for establishing new practices will be in small towns and expanding suburbs, although starting a practice will remain risky and expensive.
IP	Marketing research analysts			X	X	X	X		X					X							X		X			X	31,000	1 to 3	Faster than average growth. Best opportunities for applicants with graduate training in marketing research or statistics.
SIP	Personnel and labor relations workers			X	X	X				X	X			X		X							X				323,000	16 to 21	Faster than average growth as employers seek to raise productivity through training and development and other employee benefit programs. Keen competition for jobs in labor relations.
PC	Public relations workers			X	X	X	X		X				X	X					X		X		X		X	X	91,000	18 to 26	Growth about average. Competition for jobs likely to be keen especially during economic downturns.
ID	Purchasing agents			X	X	X			X					X	X	X					X		X		X	X	408,000	16 to 24	Average growth. Excellent job opportunities for persons with master's degrees in business administration.

SERVICE OCCUPATIONS

	OCCUPATION	1	2	3	4	5	6	7	8	9	10	11	12	13	14	15	16	17	18	19	20	21	22	23	24	25	ESTIMATED EMPLOYMENT – 1990	RANGE OF POSSIBLE CHANGE IN EMPLOYMENT (HUNDREDS) 1990-2000	EMPLOYMENT PROSPECTS
SP	Bartenders					X					X X				X			X X									414,000	19 to 26	Faster than average growth expected.

Column headings (1–25): Jobs widely scattered; Jobs concentrated in locations; Work with things; Work with ideas; Help people; Work with people; Able to see physical results of work; Opportunity for self-expression; Work as part of a team; Work independently; Work closely supervised; Direct activity of others; Generally confined to work area; Overtime or shift work required; Outdoors; High level of responsibility; Requires physical stamina; Work with detail; Repetitious work; Motivate others; Competitive; High School diploma; Technical school or apprenticeship; Junior college; College degree.

76 *How to Choose the Right Career*

SERVICE OCCUPATIONS

	OCCUPATION	1 High School diploma	2 Technical school or apprenticeship	3 Junior college	4 College degree	5 Jobs widely scattered	6 Jobs concentrated in locations	7 Work with things	8 Work with ideas	9 Help people	10 Work with people	11 Able to see physical results of work	12 Opportunity for self-expression	13 Work as part of a team	14 Work independently	15 Work closely supervised	16 Direct activity of others	17 Generally confined to work area	18 Outdoors	19 Overtime or shift work required	20 High level of responsibility	21 Requires physical stamina	22 Work with detail	23 Repetitious work	24 Motivate others	25 Competitive	ESTIMATED EMPLOYMENT – 1990	RANGE OF POSSIBLE CHANGE IN EMPLOYMENT (HUNDREDS) 1990-2000	EMPLOYMENT PROSPECTS
BI	Cooks and chefs	X	X				X	X		X	X	X		X	X	X	X				X	X	X				2,800,000	21 to 25	Employment expected to increase faster than average as population grows and people dine out more. Most starting jobs are available in small restaurants, school cafeterias, and other eating places where food preparation is relatively simple.
BD	Hotel housekeepers and assistants									X	X						X			X	X					X	138,000	21 to 39	Employment expected to grow much faster than average. Best opportunities in newly built hotels and motels.
BP	Meatcutters*	X A						X				X					X	X		X		X		X		X	368,000	11 to 18	Declining because of practice of cutting and wrapping meat for several stores at one location and changes in consumers' use of meat.
BP	Waiters and waitresses									X	X			X				X		X		X					1,800,000	19 to 28	Faster than average growth expected.

PERSONAL SERVICE OCCUPATIONS

	OCCUPATION	1	2	3	4	5	6	7	8	9	10	11	12	13	14	15	16	17	18	19	20	21	22	23	24	25			
BP	Barbers	X				X				X	X	X						X					X				76,000	3 to 7	Most openings will result from replacement needs. Better opportunities for hairstylists than for conventional barbers.
BP	Bellhops and bell captains					X				X	X					X				X		X					32,000	9 to 21	Faster than average growth expected. Best opportunities in motels, small hotels, and resort areas open only part of the year.

The Career Finder 77

ADMINISTRATIVE AND RELATED OCCUPATIONS

Column headers (Type of work and co-workers):
1. High School diploma
2. Technical school or apprenticeship
3. Junior college
4. College degree
5. Jobs widely scattered
6. Jobs concentrated in locations
7. Work with things
8. Work with ideas
9. Help people
10. Work with people
11. Able to see physical results of work
12. Opportunity for self-expression
13. Work as part of a team
14. Work independently
15. Work closely supervised
16. Direct activity of others
17. Generally confined to work area
18. Overtime or shift work required
19. Outdoors
20. High level of responsibility
21. Requires physical stamina
22. Work with detail
23. Repetitious work
24. Motivate others
25. Competitive

Code	Occupation	1	2	3	4	5	6	7	8	9	10	11	12	13	14	15	16	17	18	19	20	21	22	23	24	25	Estimated Employment 1990	Range of Possible Change (Hundreds) 1990–2000	Employment Prospects
DI	Accountants				X	X			X						X			X					X	X			963,000	25 to 34	Employment expected to increase faster than average as managers rely more on accounting information to make business decisions. College graduates will be in greater demand than applicants who lack this training.
CP	Advertising workers				X	X	X		X										X		X		X		X	X	108,000	6 to 9	Employment expected to grow due to increased number of products and services advertised.
PD	Buyers				X	X			X					X	X		X				X		X		X	X	207,000	19 to 21	Slower than average growth. Keen competition anticipated because merchandising attracts numbers of college graduates.
PD	City managers				X	X			X	X				X	X		X				X		X				3,500	1 to 2	Competition will be keen, even for persons with graduate degrees in public administration.
SP	College student personnel workers				X	X				X	X				X		X	X			X				X		56,000	1 to 2	Competition for jobs expected due to tighter budgets in public and private colleges.
DI	Credit managers	X													X		X	X			X		X	X			55,000	8 to 12	Employment expected to grow more slowly than average as centralization of credit operations increases.

78 *How to Choose the Right Career*

PERSONAL SERVICE OCCUPATIONS

	OCCUPATION	1 High School diploma	2 Technical school or apprenticeship	3 Junior college	4 College degree	5 Jobs widely scattered	6 Jobs concentrated in locations	7 Work with things	8 Work with ideas	9 Help people	10 Work with people	11 Able to see physical results of work	12 Opportunity for self-expression	13 Work as part of a team	14 Work independently	15 Work closely supervised	16 Direct activity of others	17 Generally confined to work area	18 Overtime or shift work required	19 Outdoors	20 High level of responsibility	21 Requires physical stamina	22 Work with detail	23 Repetitious work	24 Motivate others	25 Competitive	ESTIMATED EMPLOYMENT – 1990	RANGE OF POSSIBLE CHANGE IN EMPLOYMENT (HUNDREDS) 1990-2000	EMPLOYMENT PROSPECTS
SC	Cosmetologists	T				X					X	X		X	X	X											649,000	21 to 29	Employment expected to grow about as fast as average as demand for beauty shop services rises. Opportunities for part-time work should be very good.
IS	FBI special agents*				+	X					X			X	X						X	X	X				11,000	1 to 2	Rising as FBI responsibilities grow. Traditionally low turnover rate.
BS	Firefighters*	X					X	X			X			X					X		X	X					291,000	17 to 19	Employment expected to increase more slowly than average. Keen competition for jobs in urban areas; better opportunities in smaller communities.
BS	Guards*					X					X				X			X	X		X	X					795,000	23 to 34	Faster than average growth. Best opportunities in guard and security agencies and in night-shift jobs.
BS	Police officers*	X					X				X			X	X				X	X	X	X	X				437,750	17 to 19	Faster than average growth. Best prospects for applicants with college training in law enforcement.
BS	State police officers*	X					X				X			X	X				X	X	X	X	X				51,500	13 to 15	Tight budgets will cause competition for jobs in most states.
ID	Health and regulatory inspectors (government)*	(1)	(1)	(1)					X						X						X		X	X	X		112,000	12 to 14	Below average.

TYPE OF WORK AND CO-WORKERS

The Career Finder 79

Column Headers

TYPE OF WORK AND CO-WORKERS (columns 1–25):
1. High School diploma
2. Technical school or apprenticeship
3. Junior college
4. College degree
5. Jobs widely scattered
6. Jobs concentrated in locations
7. Work with things
8. Work with ideas
9. Help people
10. Work with people
11. Able to see physical results of work
12. Opportunity for self-expression
13. Work as part of a team
14. Work independently
15. Work closely supervised
16. Direct activity of others
17. Generally confined to work area
18. Overtime or shift work required
19. Outdoors
20. High level of responsibility
21. Requires physical stamina
22. Work with detail
23. Repetitious work
24. Motivate others
25. Competitive

Additional columns: ESTIMATED EMPLOYMENT – 1990 | RANGE OF POSSIBLE CHANGE IN EMPLOYMENT (HUNDREDS) 1990-2000 | EMPLOYMENT PROSPECTS

PERSONAL SERVICE OCCUPATIONS

Code	Occupation	1	2	3	4	5	6	7	8	9	10	11	12	13	14	15	16	17	18	19	20	21	22	23	24	25	Est. Emp. 1990	Range of Change	Employment Prospects
IB	Construction inspectors	X	T			X			X						X					X	X	X	X				56,000	21 to 23	Average growth expected. Best opportunities for college graduates and persons experienced as carpenters, electricians, or plumbers.

OTHER SERVICE OCCUPATIONS

Code	Occupation	1	2	3	4	5	6	7	8	9	10	11	12	13	14	15	16	17	18	19	20	21	22	23	24	25	Est. Emp. 1990	Range of Change	Employment Prospects
BD	Mail carriers					X		X		X	X				X		X			X	X						380,000	1 to 2	Average growth expected.
DP	Telephone operators	X				X		X		X					X				X X			X					330,000	14 to 15	Declining due to increased direct dialing and technological improvements.

EDUCATION AND RELATED OCCUPATIONS

TEACHING OCCUPATIONS

Code	Occupation	1	2	3	4	5	6	7	8	9	10	11	12	13	14	15	16	17	18	19	20	21	22	23	24	25	Est. Emp. 1990	Range of Change	Employment Prospects
SP	Kindergarten and elementary school teachers				+	X				X	X	X		X	X		X			X	X				X X		1,359,000	13 to 17	Employment expected to grow as fast as average. Job prospects may improve due to rising enrollments. Outlook for qualified elementary school teachers is likely to be good unless the number of job seekers increases.

80 How to Choose the Right Career

EDUCATIONAL AND RELATED OCCUPATIONS

TEACHING OCCUPATIONS

	OCCUPATION	1 College degree	2 Junior college	3 Technical school or apprenticeship	4 High School diploma	5 Jobs concentrated in locations	6 Jobs widely scattered	7 Work with things	8 Work with ideas	9 Help people	10 Work with people	11 Able to see physical results of work	12 Opportunity for self-expression	13 Work as part of a team	14 Work independently	15 Work closely supervised	16 Direct activity of others	17 Generally confined to work area	18 Overtime or shift work required	19 Outdoors	20 High level of responsibility	21 Requires physical stamina	22 Work with detail	23 Repetitious work	24 Motivate others	25 Competitive	ESTIMATED EMPLOYMENT – 1990	RANGE OF POSSIBLE CHANGE IN EMPLOYMENT (HUNDREDS) 1990-2000	EMPLOYMENT PROSPECTS
SP	Secondary school teachers	+							X	+	X		X	X	X		X	X	X		X		X		X		1,164,000	1 to 2	Keen competition expected due to new college graduates qualified to teach. Generally, favorable opportunities will exist for persons qualified to teach special education, vocational subjects, mathematics, and the natural and physical sciences.
SI	College and university faculty	+							X	+	X		X	X	X		X	X	X		X		X		X		691,000[5]	1 to 3	Employment expected to decline due to decreasing enrollments and budgetary constraints. Keen competition in all but a few disciplines, and many of the available openings will be part-time or short term. Good job prospects for mathematics, engineering, and computer science faculty.

LIBRARY OCCUPATIONS

	OCCUPATION																												
DI	Librarians	+					X			+	X			X					X		X		X				143,000	3 to 5	Little change expected in employment in school, public, and academic libraries due to declining enrollments and budget constraints. Keen competition for jobs. Best opportunities for librarians with scientific or technical qualifications.
BD	Library technicians and assistants		T								X			X				X					X				54,000	1 to 2	Little change expected in employment. Best job prospects in special libraries.

TYPE OF WORK AND CO-WORKERS

The Career Finder 81

SALES OCCUPATIONS

	OCCUPATION	1 Jobs widely scattered	2 Jobs concentrated in locations	3 Work with things	4 Work with ideas	5 Help people	6 Work with people	7 Able to see physical results of work	8 Opportunity for self-expression	9 Work as part of a team	10 Work independently	11 Work closely supervised	12 Direct activity of others	13 Generally confined to work area	14 Overtime or shift work required	15 Outdoors	16 High level of responsibility	17 Requires physical stamina	18 Work with detail	19 Repetitious work	20 Motivate others	21 Competitive	22 College degree	23 Junior college	24 Technical school or apprenticeship	25 High School diploma	ESTIMATED EMPLOYMENT – 1990	RANGE OF POSSIBLE CHANGE IN EMPLOYMENT (HUNDREDS) 1990-2000	EMPLOYMENT PROSPECTS
PI	Automobile parts counter workers	X				X		X		X	X				X											X	95,000	18 to 28	Better than average due to increasing demand for new accessories and replacement parts.
S PI	Automobile sales workers	X				X				X	X				X				X						X	X	133,000	19 to 21	Slower than average growth. Job openings may fluctuate because sales are affected by changing economic conditions.
PI	Manufacturers and wholesale sales workers				+	X				X	X				X				X		X		X		X	X	1,883,000	15 to 24	Employment expected to grow faster than average. Good opportunities for persons with product knowledge and sales ability.
CP	Models						X				X			X	X				X			X				X	83,000	1 to 2	Better than average due to rising advertising expenditures and greater sales of clothing and accessories. Because occupation is so small and the glamour of modeling attracts many, competition should be keen.
PD	Real estate agents and brokers	X T				X				X	X				X				X		X		X		X	X	540,000	19 to 23	Slower than average growth. Highly competitive. Best prospects for college graduates and transferees from other sales jobs.
PI	Retail trade sales workers					X				X	X				X				X						X	X	3,800,300	21 to 23	Faster than average growth. High turnover should create excellent opportunities for full-time, part-time, and temporary work.

TYPE OF WORK AND CO-WORKERS

82 *How to Choose the Right Career*

Column headers (1–25):
1. High School diploma
2. Technical school or apprenticeship
3. Junior college
4. College degree
5. Jobs widely scattered
6. Jobs concentrated in locations
7. Work with things
8. Work with ideas
9. Help people
10. Work with people
11. Able to see physical results of work
12. Opportunity for self-expression
13. Work as part of a team
14. Work independently
15. Work closely supervised
16. Direct activity of others
17. Generally confined to work area
18. Overtime or shift work required
19. Outdoors
20. High level of responsibility
21. Requires physical stamina
22. Work with detail
23. Repetitious work
24. Motivate others
25. Competitive

SALES OCCUPATIONS

	Occupation	1	2	3	4	5	6	7	8	9	10	11	12	13	14	15	16	17	18	19	20	21	22	23	24	25	Estimated Employment – 1990	Range of Possible Change in Employment (Hundreds) 1990-2000	Employment Prospects
PB	Route drivers					X					X				X	X			X			X			X	X	230,000	21 to 27	Several thousand openings will result annually from replacement needs. Best opportunities for applicants who have sales experience and good driving records.
PD	Securities sales and financial services workers				+	X			X		X	X		X	X	X			X			X			X	X	220,000	21 to 44	Employment expected to grow slower than average.
PD	Travel agents		T							X	X	X				X					X						142,000	29 to 33	Growth expected. Highly competitive. Opportunities sensitive to economic changes.
PD	Wholesale trade sales workers	X				X					X				X	X			X		X		X		X	X	1,883,000	19 to 30	Growth faster than average. Good opportunities for persons with product knowledge and sales ability.

CONSTRUCTION OCCUPATIONS

	Occupation	1	2	3	4	5	6	7	8	9	10	11	12	13	14	15	16	17	18	19	20	21	22	23	24	25	Estimated Employment – 1990	Range of Possible Change in Employment (Hundreds) 1990-2000	Employment Prospects
BD	Bricklayers, stonemasons, and marble setters*	A				X		X				X		X		X				X		X					167,000	33 to 39	Average growth expected. Job openings should be plentiful except during economic downturns.
BD	Carpenters*	X				X		X				X		X		X				X		X					1,106,000	19 to 22	Average. Sensitive to economic conditions.
BD	Cement masons and terrazzo workers*	X				X		X				X		X		X		X	X	X		X					114,000	33 to 37	Average growth expected.

The Career Finder 83

CONSTRUCTION OCCUPATIONS

	OCCUPATION	1 High School diploma	2 Technical school or apprenticeship	3 Junior college	4 College degree	5 Jobs widely scattered	6 Jobs concentrated in locations	7 Work with things	8 Work with ideas	9 Help people	10 Work with people	11 Able to see physical results of work	12 Opportunity for self-expression	13 Work as part of a team	14 Work independently	15 Work closely supervised	16 Direct activity of others	17 Generally confined to work area	18 Overtime or shift work required	19 Outdoors	20 High level of responsibility	21 Requires physical stamina	22 Work with detail	23 Repetitious work	24 Motivate others	25 Competitive	ESTIMATED EMPLOYMENT – 1990	RANGE OF POSSIBLE CHANGE IN EMPLOYMENT (HUNDREDS) 1990-2000	EMPLOYMENT PROSPECTS
BD	Construction laborers*					X		X			X	X				X		X		X		X					2,430,000	22 to 32	Employment expected to grow about as fast as average. Job openings should be plentiful except during economic downturns.
BI	Electricians	A						X			X	X		X				X				X					542,000	20 to 28	Average, as more electricians are needed to install electrical fixtures and wiring in new and renovated buildings.
BI	Elevator constructors*		X					X			X	X		X				X				X					13,000	17 to 23	Average growth expected.
BD	Floor covering installers	X	A					X			X	X		X		X						X					56,000	21 to 23	Faster than average growth. Best opportunities for those able to install carpeting and resilient flooring.
BD	Glaziers*	X						X			X	X				X				X		X					49,000	20 to 25	Average as popularity in glass in building design continues.
BD	Insulation workers*	X						X			X	X		X		X						X		X			65,000	31 to 40	Average growth expected as energy saving insulation is installed in homes and businesses.
BD	Ironworkers*	X						X			X	X		X		X				X	X	X		X			91,000	19 to 21	Employment expected to increase as fast as average due to demand for office and industrial buildings, transmission towers, and other structures.

84 *How to Choose the Right Career*

CONSTRUCTION OCCUPATIONS

	OCCUPATION	1 High School diploma	2 Technical school or apprenticeship	3 Junior college	4 College degree	5 Jobs widely scattered	6 Jobs concentrated in locations	7 Work with things	8 Work with ideas	9 Help people	10 Work with people	11 Able to see physical results of work	12 Opportunity for self-expression	13 Work as part of a team	14 Work independently	15 Work closely supervised	16 Direct activity of others	17 Generally confined to work area	18 Overtime or shift work required	19 Outdoors	20 High level of responsibility	21 Requires physical stamina	22 Work with detail	23 Repetitious work	24 Motivate others	25 Competitive	ESTIMATED EMPLOYMENT – 1990	RANGE OF POSSIBLE CHANGE IN EMPLOYMENT (HUNDREDS) 1990-2000	EMPLOYMENT PROSPECTS
BD	Operating engineers (construction machinery operators)	X	T					X			X	X				X				X	X	X					244,000	17 to 21	Employment expected to grow as fast as average due to construction activity. Job opportunities should be plentiful except during economic downturns.
BS	Paperhangers* and painters		X					X			X	X				X				X		X					431,000	17 to 21	Average growth expected.
BD	Plasterers		X					X			X	X		X		X						X					27,000	13 to 17	Employment will grow more slowly than average.
BI	Plumbers and pipe fitters		A					X			X	X				X				X		X					396,000	21 to 27	Employment expected to grow about as fast as average as a result of construction activity and the need to repair and modernize existing plumbing and piping.
BI	Roofers*	X						X			X	X				X				X	X	X					123,000	17 to 23	Employment expected to grow as fast as average as a result of new construction and the need to repair existing roofs. Demand for dampproofing and waterproofing also will stimulate employment.
BD	Sheet-metal workers	X	A					X			X	X				X		X				X					97,000	20 to 22	Average due to need for air conditioning and heating ducts and other sheet-metal products.

The Career Finder **85**

Column headers (TYPE OF WORK AND CO-WORKERS):
1. High School diploma
2. Technical school or apprenticeship
3. Junior college
4. College degree
5. Jobs widely scattered
6. Jobs concentrated in locations
7. Work with things
8. Work with ideas
9. Help people
10. Work with people
11. Able to see physical results of work
12. Opportunity for self-expression
13. Work as part of a team
14. Work independently
15. Work closely supervised
16. Direct activity of others
17. Generally confined to work area
18. Overtime or shift work required
19. Outdoors
20. High level of responsibility
21. Requires physical stamina
22. Work with detail
23. Repetitious work
24. Motivate others
25. Competitive

CONSTRUCTION OCCUPATIONS

	OCCUPATION	1	2	3	4	5	6	7	8	9	10	11	12	13	14	15	16	17	18	19	20	21	22	23	24	25	ESTIMATED EMPLOYMENT – 1990	RANGE OF POSSIBLE CHANGE IN EMPLOYMENT (HUNDREDS) 1990-2000	EMPLOYMENT PROSPECTS
BD	Tile setters		A			X		X	X			X				X		X					X				26,000	36 to 48	Employment expected to increase faster than average as tile is increasingly used in new kitchens, bathrooms, hallways, and recreation areas.

AIR TRANSPORTATION OCCUPATIONS

	OCCUPATION	1	2	3	4	5	6	7	8	9	10	11	12	13	14	15	16	17	18	19	20	21	22	23	24	25	ESTIMATED EMPLOYMENT – 1990	RANGE OF POSSIBLE CHANGE IN EMPLOYMENT (HUNDREDS) 1990-2000	EMPLOYMENT PROSPECTS
ID	Air traffic controllers	X	T				X							X			X	X	X		X		X				24,000	16 to 19	Best opportunities for college graduates with experience as controller pilots or navigators.
BI	Aircraft mechanics*	X	T				X	X						X			X	X	X	X			X				110,000	40 to 50	Good opportunities in general aviation; keen competition for airline jobs; opportunities in federal government depending upon defense spending.
IB	Airplane pilots	X	T				X	X						X			X	X	X		X	X	X				83,000	15 to 23	Employment expected to grow as fast as average due to increased air travel. Applicants are likely to face keen competition for available jobs. Best opportunities for ex-military pilots and college graduates with flying experience.
SP	Flight attendants	X					X			X	X						X		X			X					88,000	15 to 22	Faster than average growth but highly competitive.

86 *How to Choose the Right Career*

			1	2	3	4	5	6	7	8	9	10	11	12	13	14	15	16	17	18	19	20	21	22	23	24	25	ESTIMATED EMPLOYMENT – 1990	RANGE OF POSSIBLE CHANGE IN EMPLOYMENT (HUNDREDS) 1990-2000	EMPLOYMENT PROSPECTS

Column legend (TYPE OF WORK AND CO-WORKERS):
1. High School diploma
2. Technical school or apprenticeship
3. Junior college
4. College degree
5. Jobs widely scattered
6. Jobs concentrated in locations
7. Work with things
8. Work with ideas
9. Help people
10. Work with people
11. Able to see physical results of work
12. Opportunity for self-expression
13. Work as part of a team
14. Work independently
15. Work closely supervised
16. Direct activity of others
17. Generally confined to work area
18. Overtime or shift work required
19. Outdoors
20. High level of responsibility
21. Requires physical stamina
22. Work with detail
23. Repetitious work
24. Motivate others
25. Competitive

MERCHANT MARINE OCCUPATIONS

	OCCUPATION	1	2	3	4	5	6	7	8	9	10	11	12	13	14	15	16	17	18	19	20	21	22	23	24	25	Est. Emp.	Range	Employment Prospects
PI	Merchant marine officers*	T		X			X		X						X		X		X		X	X					26,800	2 to 4	Little change in employment expected as size of nation's fleet remains fairly constant. Job prospects good in offshore mineral and oil exploration.
BI	Merchant marine sailors*						X	X						X		X			X		X	X	X				28,400	–1 to –3	Declining as smaller crews operate new ships.

DRIVING OCCUPATIONS

	OCCUPATION	1	2	3	4	5	6	7	8	9	10	11	12	13	14	15	16	17	18	19	20	21	22	23	24	25	Est. Emp.	Range	Employment Prospects
BP	Intercity and local transit busdrivers							X			X			X							X						506,000	21 to 27	Average.
BD	Local and long distance truck drivers					X		X							X			X		X	X	X					2,600,000	23 to 31	Stiff competition is likely for available jobs in this high-paying occupation.

SCIENTIFIC AND TECHNICAL OCCUPATIONS

CONSERVATION OCCUPATIONS

	OCCUPATION	1	2	3	4	5	6	7	8	9	10	11	12	13	14	15	16	17	18	19	20	21	22	23	24	25	Est. Emp.	Range	Employment Prospects
BI	Foresters*				+	X		X						X			X			X	X	X					27,000	9 to 14	Employment expected to grow more slowly than average. Applicants are likely to face competition. Job prospects are better for persons with advanced degrees. Job growth dependent upon government budgets.

The Career Finder **87**

OCCUPATION	Education	Type of Work and Co-Workers (1-25)	Estimated Employment 1990	Range of Possible Change in Employment (Hundreds) 1990-2000	Employment Prospects
SCIENTIFIC AND TECHNICAL OCCUPATIONS					
CONSERVATION OCCUPATIONS					
Forestry technicians*	BI	1:X, 3:X, 4:X, 6:X, 11:X, 12:X, 17:X, 18:X, 20:X	13,500	4 to 5	Average as use of technology in forest industry increases. Even applicants with specialized school training may face competition, however.
Range managers*	BI	3:+, 5:X, 6:X, 8:X, 11:X, 12:X, 14:X, 19:X, 20:X	4,600	1 to 3	Average as use of rangelands for grazing, recreation, and wildlife habitats increases.
Soil conservationists	BI	4:X, 5:X, 6:X, 8:X, 11:X, 12:X, 14:X, 19:X, 20:X, 21:X, 22:X	7,400	1 to 2	Average. Prospects better in non-government organizations.
ENGINEERS					
Aerospace Engineers	IB	3:X, 6:X, 8:X, 11:X, 12:X, 16:X, 20:X, 22:X	78,000	21 to 27	Above average due to increased expenditures on commercial and defense programs.
Agricultural Engineers	IB	3:X, 6:X, 8:X, 11:X, 12:X, 16:X, 19:X, 22:X	25,000	22 to 27	Above average because of increasing demand for agricultural products, modernization of farm operations, and conservation.
Biomedical Engineers	IB	3:X, 6:X, 8:X, 11:X, 12:X, 16:X, 22:X	14,700	7 to 8	Faster than average growth. Increased research funds could create new jobs in instrumentation and systems for delivery of health services.
Ceramic Engineers	IB	3:X, 6:X, 8:X, 11:X, 12:X, 16:X, 22:X	16,900	2 to 3	Above average as a result of need to develop ceramic materials for nuclear energy, electronics, defense, and medical science.

88 *How to Choose the Right Career*

ENGINEERS

	OCCUPATION	Education	Type of Work and Co-workers (columns 1-22)	Estimated Employment 1990	Range of Possible Change in Employment (Hundreds) 1990-2000	Employment Prospects
IB	Chemical Engineers	College degree (22)	4, 8, 11, 12, 13, 16 (X)	49,000	17 to 19	Average growth expected. Growing complexity and automation of chemical processes will require additional chemical engineers to design, build, and maintain plants and equipment.
IB	Civil Engineers	College degree (22)	4, 5, 6, 8, 11, 12, 13, 16, 20 (X)	186,000	21 to 23	Above average as a result of need for housing, industrial buildings, electric power generating plants, and transportation systems. Work related to environmental pollution and energy self-sufficiency also will create openings.
IB	Electrical Engineers	College degree (22)	4, 8, 11, 12, 13, 16 (X)	439,000	37 to 43	Growing demand for computers, communications equipment, military electronics, consumer goods, and power generation also should create many openings.
IB	Industrial Engineers	College degree (22, 24)	4, 5, 8, 11, 12, 13, 16, 20 (X)	132,000	27 to 38	Better than average due to industrial growth, increasing complexity of industrial operations, expansion of automated processes, and greater emphasis on scientific management and safety engineering.
IB	Mechanical Engineers	College degree (22)	4 (C); 5, 8, 11, 12, 13, 16 (X)	225,000	29 to 43	Average due to growing demand for industrial machinery and machine tools. Need to develop new energy systems and to solve environmental pollution problems also will create openings.

Column key (Type of Work and Co-workers): 1. Jobs widely scattered; 2. Jobs concentrated in locations; 3. Work with things; 4. Work with ideas; 5. Help people; 6. Work with people; 7. Able to see physical results of work; 8. Opportunity for self-expression; 9. Work as part of a team; 10. Work independently; 11. Work closely supervised; 12. Direct activity of others; 13. Generally confined to work area; 14. Overtime or shift work required; 15. Outdoors; 16. High level of responsibility; 17. Requires physical stamina; 18. Work with detail; 19. Repetitious work; 20. Motivate others; 21. Competitive; 22. High School diploma / Technical school or apprenticeship / Junior college / College degree.

TYPE OF WORK AND CO-WORKERS	OCCUPATION	1 High School diploma	2 Technical school or apprenticeship	3 Junior college	4 College degree	5 Jobs widely scattered	6 Jobs concentrated in locations	7 Work with things	8 Work with ideas	9 Help people	10 Work with people	11 Able to see physical results of work	12 Opportunity for self-expression	13 Work as part of a team	14 Work independently	15 Work closely supervised	16 Direct activity of others	17 Generally confined to work area	18 Overtime or shift work required	19 Outdoors	20 High level of responsibility	21 Requires physical stamina	22 Work with detail	23 Repetitious work	24 Motivate others	25 Competitive	ESTIMATED EMPLOYMENT – 1990	RANGE OF POSSIBLE CHANGE IN EMPLOYMENT (HUNDREDS) 1990-2000	EMPLOYMENT PROSPECTS
ENGINEERS																													
IB	Metallurgical Engineers				+		X		X			X	X	X			X						X				19,000	31 to 37	Average growth expected due to need to develop new metals and alloys, adapt current ones to new needs, and develop new ways to recycle solid wastes.
IB	Mining Engineers				+		X		X			X	X	X			X			X	X		X				5,300	16 to 21	Slower than average due to uncertain energy-needs projections.
ENVIRONMENTAL SCIENTISTS																													
IB	Geologists				+		X		X				X		X								X				42,000	23 to 27	Above average as domestic mineral exploration increases. Good opportunities for persons with degrees in geology.
IB	Geophysicists				+		X		X				X		X								X				15,000	13 to 17	Above average as petroleum and mining companies need additional geophysicists able to use sophisticated electronic techniques in exploration. Very good opportunities for graduates in geophysics or related areas.
IB	Meteorologists				+		X		X				X		X				X				X				6,200	2 to 4	Little change in employment expected.
IB	Oceanographers				+		X		X				X	X			X			X			X				3,200	1 to 3	Average growth is expected, competition for openings is likely. Best opportunities for persons who have Ph.D.'s; those with less education may be limited to research assistant and technician jobs.

90 *How to Choose the Right Career*

LIFE SCIENCE OCCUPATIONS

	OCCUPATION	4. Help people	5. Work with people	8. Work as part of a team	12. Direct activity of others	14. Overtime or shift work required	22.	ESTIMATED EMPLOYMENT – 1990	RANGE OF POSSIBLE CHANGE IN EMPLOYMENT (HUNDREDS) 1990-2000	EMPLOYMENT PROSPECTS
IB	Biochemists	+	X	X	X		X	16,000	17 to 22	Average due to increased funds for biochemical research and development. Favorable opportunities for advanced degree holders.
IB	Agricultural and biological scientists	+	X	X	X	X	X	133,000	22 to 27	Employment expected to grow as fast as average due to increasing expenditures for medical and agricultural research. Good opportunities for persons with advanced degrees.

MATHEMATICS OCCUPATIONS

	OCCUPATION	4	5	8	12	14	17	22	EST. EMPL.	RANGE	EMPLOYMENT PROSPECTS
ID	Mathematicians	+	X	X	X	X	X	X	49,000	11 to 14	Employment expected to grow at an average rate. Favorable job prospects expected for Ph.D.'s in industry and in college faculty positions at the undergraduate level. However, competition is expected for jobs involving theoretical research. Competition for mathematician jobs likely among those without a Ph.D., although favorable job prospects are expected in related science, engineering, and computer occupations.
ID	Statisticians	+		X	X X		X	X	26,000	13 to 17	Faster than average growth. Persons combining knowledge of statistics with a field of application, such as economics, have favorable job opportunities.

Column headers (TYPE OF WORK AND CO-WORKERS):
1. High School diploma
2. Technical school or apprenticeship
3. Junior college
4. College degree
5. Jobs widely scattered
6. Jobs concentrated in locations
7. Work with things
8. Work with ideas
9. Help people
10. Work with people
11. Able to see physical results of work
12. Opportunity for self-expression
13. Work as part of a team
14. Work independently
15. Work closely supervised
16. Direct activity of others
17. Generally confined to work area
18. Outdoors
19. Overtime or shift work required
20. High level of responsibility
21. Requires physical stamina
22. Work with detail
23. Repetitious work
24. Motivate others
25. Competitive

The Career Finder

PHYSICAL SCIENTISTS

	OCCUPATION	1 Jobs widely scattered	2 Jobs concentrated in locations	3 Work with things	4 Work with ideas	5 Help people	6 Work with people	7 Able to see physical results of work	8 Opportunity for self-expression	9 Work as part of a team	10 Work independently	11 Work closely supervised	12 Direct activity of others	13 Generally confined to work area	14 Overtime or shift work required	15 Outdoors	16 High level of responsibility	17 Requires physical stamina	18 Work with detail	19 Repetitious work	20 Motivate others	21 Competitive	ESTIMATED EMPLOYMENT – 1990	RANGE OF POSSIBLE CHANGE IN EMPLOYMENT (HUNDREDS) 1990-2000	EMPLOYMENT PROSPECTS
IC	Astronomers				+		X		X				X		X								2,000	1 to 3	Limited with slight increases in funds for basic research. Competitive.
IC	Chemists				+		X		X				X		X								99,000	15 to 19	Employment expected to grow as fast as average as a result of increasing demand for new products, manufacturing efficiency, and energy conservation. Good opportunities are expected at all degree levels.
IC	Food technologists				+		X		X				X		X								15,000	13 to 14	Employment expected to grow more slowly than average due to slow growth of the food processing industry.
IC	Physicists				+		X		X				X		X								32,000	5 to 9	Although employment will grow at about average rate, very good job opportunities are expected for persons with advanced degrees in physics. Persons with only a bachelor's degree will face competition for jobs as physicists, but should have favorable prospects for jobs as engineers, computer scientists, and technicians.

OTHER SCIENTIFIC AND TECHNICAL OCCUPATIONS

	OCCUPATION	1	2	3	4	5	6	7	8	9	10	11	12	13	14	15	16	17	18	19	20	21	EST. EMP.	RANGE	EMPLOYMENT PROSPECTS
BI	Broadcast technicians	X	T			X		X						X			X		X		X	X	27,000	11 to 13	Prospects best in smaller cities. Highly competitive. Growth slower than average.

92 *How to Choose the Right Career*

Column headers (1–25):
1. High School diploma
2. Technical school or apprenticeship
3. Junior college
4. College degree
5. Jobs widely scattered
6. Jobs concentrated in locations
7. Work with things
8. Work with ideas
9. Help people
10. Work with people
11. Able to see physical results of work
12. Opportunity for self-expression
13. Work as part of a team
14. Work independently
15. Work closely supervised
16. Direct activity of others
17. Generally confined to work area
18. Overtime or shift work required
19. Outdoors
20. High level of responsibility
21. Requires physical stamina
22. Work with detail
23. Repetitious work
24. Motivate others
25. Competitive

OTHER SCIENTIFIC AND TECHNICAL OCCUPATIONS

	Occupation	1	2	3	4	5	6	7	8	9	10	11	12	13	14	15	16	17	18	19	20	21	22	23	24	25	Est. Employment 1990	Range of Change (hundreds) 1990–2000	Employment Prospects
BS	Drafters	X	T	X			X	X	X					X		X		X					X				319,000	21 to 24	Average growth is expected due to increasing complexity of design problems. Best prospects for those with associate degrees or training in computer-aided drafting.
ID	Surveyors and surveying technicians	X	T				X		X					X		X			X	X			X				100,000	21 to 27	Employment expected to grow about as fast as average due to increased construction activity.

MECHANICS AND REPAIRERS

	Occupation	1	2	3	4	5	6	7	8	9	10	11	12	13	14	15	16	17	18	19	20	21	22	23	24	25	Est. Employment 1990	Range of Change (hundreds) 1990–2000	Employment Prospects
BI	Central office craft occupations* (telephone repairers)	X					X	X				X		X				X	X				X	X			113,000	–3 to –5	Employment expected to show little growth and may decline as more efficient electronic switching systems replace electro-mechanical ones.
BI	Line installers and cable splicers*	X					X	X						X		X		X	X			X	X	X			231,000	11 to 21	Some decline in employment is expected as technological improvements limit growth. Employment may increase, however, if modernization programs are accelerated.
BI	Telephone installers and repairers*	X					X	X		X				X				X	X			X	X	X			58,000	9 to 11	Very little growth expected.

The Career Finder 93

OTHER MECHANICS AND REPAIRERS

	OCCUPATION	1	2	3	4	5	6	7	8	9	10	11	12	13	14	15	16	17	18	19	20	21	22	23	24	25	ESTIMATED EMPLOYMENT – 1990	RANGE OF POSSIBLE CHANGE IN EMPLOYMENT (HUNDREDS) 1990-2000	EMPLOYMENT PROSPECTS
IB	Air-conditioning, refrigeration, and heating mechanics*	X	T			X		X				X			X				X								225,000	23 to 27	Employment expected to increase about as fast as average. Beginning mechanics may face competition for the highest paying jobs. Graduates of training programs that emphasize hands-on experience will have the best opportunities.
IB	Appliance repairers					X		X				X			X												79,000	16 to 25	Average.
BI	Automobile body repairers*		A			X		X				X			X			X				X					214,000	19 to 22	Faster than average growth expected.
BI	Automobile mechanics*		A			X		X				X			X			X				X					771,000	21 to 23	Average increase is expected due to growing number of automobiles. Job opportunities will be plentiful.
BD	Business machine repairers*					X		X							X								X				57,000	20 to 25	Above average as machines increase.
IB	Computer service technicians*		T			X		X				X			X					X							71,000	25 to 33	Better than average as more computer equipment is used. Very good opportunities for persons with postsecondary school training in electronics.
BI	Electric sign repairers*					X		X				X			X				X	X		X	X				15,500	2 to 4	Increasing.
BI	Farm equipment mechanics*		A			X		X							X				X	X		X					54,000	17 to 29	Increasing. Best opportunities for persons familiar with farms and farm machinery.

Column headers (1–25): 1 High School diploma; 2 Technical school or apprenticeship; 3 Junior college; 4 College degree; 5 Jobs widely scattered; 6 Jobs concentrated in locations; 7 Work with things; 8 Work with ideas; 9 Help people; 10 Work with people; 11 Able to see physical results of work; 12 Opportunity for self-expression; 13 Work as part of a team; 14 Work independently; 15 Work closely supervised; 16 Direct activity of others; 17 Generally confined to work area; 18 Overtime or shift work required; 19 Outdoors; 20 High level of responsibility; 21 Requires physical stamina; 22 Work with detail; 23 Repetitious work; 24 Motivate others; 25 Competitive

TYPE OF WORK AND CO-WORKERS

94 How to Choose the Right Career

OTHER MECHANICS AND REPAIRERS

TYPE OF WORK AND CO-WORKERS	OCCUPATION	High School diploma (1)	Technical school or apprenticeship (2)	Junior college (3)	College degree (4)	Jobs widely scattered (5)	Jobs concentrated in locations (6)	Work with things (7)	Work with ideas (8)	Help people (9)	Work with people (10)	Able to see physical results of work (11)	Opportunity for self-expression (12)	Work as part of a team (13)	Work independently (14)	Work closely supervised (15)	Direct activity of others (16)	Generally confined to work area (17)	Overtime or shift work required (18)	Outdoors (19)	High level of responsibility (20)	Requires physical stamina (21)	Work with detail (22)	Repetitious work (23)	Motivate others (24)	Competitive (25)	ESTIMATED EMPLOYMENT – 1990	RANGE OF POSSIBLE CHANGE IN EMPLOYMENT (HUNDREDS) 1990-2000	EMPLOYMENT PROSPECTS
BI	Industrial machinery repairers*	X	A			X		X			X	X			X				X								463,000	15 to 21	Average growth as more repairs will be needed to maintain growing amount of machinery used in manufacturing, coal mining, oil exploration, and other industries.
BI	Jewelers	X	A			X		X		X		X			X							X	X				35,000	15 to 19	Employment expected to grow about as fast as average as the demand for jewelry and jewelry repair increases.
BI	Piano and organ tuners and repairers	X	A				X X	X		X					X				X				X				7,500	1 to 2	Little change expected in employment. Opportunities for trainee jobs are best for individuals with work experience or vocational training.
BI	Shoe repairs	X	A			X		X		X	X	X			X	X			X					X			31,500	11 to 15	Employment expected to grow more slowly than average. Job prospects should be very good because of replacement needs. Because training is difficult to obtain, many openings are not filled.
BI	Television and radio service technicians*		T			X		X		X		X			X	X			X				X				44,000	11 to 15	Average growth expected as number of home electronic products such as television sets, video games, radios, phonographs, and tape recorders increases.
BI	Truck mechanics and bus mechanics*		A			X		X							X				X			X					269,000	22 to 27	Employment of truck mechanics expected to grow about as fast as average due to increasing use of trucks and buses.

The Career Finder

Column headers (TYPE OF WORK AND CO-WORKERS)

1. High School diploma
2. Technical school or apprenticeship
3. Junior college
4. College degree
5. Jobs widely scattered
6. Jobs concentrated in locations
7. Work with things
8. Work with ideas
9. Help people
10. Work with people
11. Able to see physical results of work
12. Opportunity for self-expression
13. Work as part of a team
14. Work independently
15. Work closely supervised
16. Direct activity of others
17. Generally confined to work area
18. Overtime or shift work required
19. Outdoors
20. High level of responsibility
21. Requires physical stamina
22. Work with detail
23. Repetitious work
24. Motivate others
25. Competitive

OTHER MECHANICS AND REPAIRERS

	Occupation	1	2	3	4	5	6	7	8	9	10	11	12	13	14	15	16	17	18	19	20	21	22	23	24	25	Estimated Employment – 1990	Range of Possible Change in Employment (Hundreds) 1990-2000	Employment Prospects
BI	Vending machine mechanics*		T				X	X				X											X				27,000	4 to 14	Little or no change through 2000.
BI	Watch repairers		T			X		X				X						X	X				X				9,500	1 to 3	Although below average, trained workers should find jobs readily available. Opportunities good for persons trained in repairing electronic watches.

HEALTH OCCUPATIONS
DENTAL OCCUPATIONS

	Occupation	1	2	3	4	5	6	7	8	9	10	11	12	13	14	15	16	17	18	19	20	21	22	23	24	25	Estimated Employment – 1990	Range of Possible Change in Employment (Hundreds) 1990-2000	Employment Prospects
IB	Dentists	X	T		+	X				X	X	X	X		X		X				X		X				167,000	14 to 17	Average.
SC	Dental assistants			X		X				X	X			X		X		X						X			166,000	30 to 33	Average growth expected. Good opportunities for full- and part-time jobs.
SC	Dental hygienists			X		X				X	X			X				X						X		X	91,000	7 to 11	Above average because of expanding population and growing awareness of importance of regular dental care.
BI	Dental laboratory technicians	X	7	7			X					X			X	X		X					X	X			51,000	11 to 17	Slower than average growth.

96 *How to Choose the Right Career*

TYPE OF WORK AND CO-WORKERS

Columns:
1. High School diploma
2. Technical school or apprenticeship
3. Junior college
4. College degree
5. Jobs widely scattered
6. Jobs concentrated in locations
7. Work with things
8. Work with ideas
9. Help people
10. Work with people
11. Able to see physical results of work
12. Opportunity for self-expression
13. Work as part of a team
14. Work independently
15. Work closely supervised
16. Direct activity of others
17. Generally confined to work area
18. Overtime or shift work required
19. Outdoors
20. High level of responsibility
21. Requires physical stamina
22. Work with detail
23. Repetitious work
24. Motivate others
25. Competitive

MEDICAL PRACTITIONERS

	Occupation	1	2	3	4	5	6	7	8	9	10	11	12	13	14	15	16	17	18	19	20	21	22	23	24	25	Est. Emp. 1990	Range of Change (hundreds) 1990-2000	Employment Prospects
IS	Chiropractors				+	X				+	X	X		X	X	X					X		X	X			36,000	11 to 15	New chiropractors may have difficulty establishing a practice due to dramatic increases in number of chiropractic graduates. Best opportunities in small towns and areas with few practitioners.
IS	Optometrists				+	X				+	X	X		X	X	X					X		X	X			37,000	11 to 19	Average growth through 2000.
IS	Physicians and osteopathic physicians*				+	X				+	X	X		X	X	X					X		X	X			535,000	11 to 30	Very favorable. New physicians should have little difficulty establishing new practices.
IS	Podiatrists				+	X				+		X		X	X	X					X		X	X			17,000	27 to 30	Opportunities for graduates to establish new practices or to enter salaried positions should be favorable.
IB	Veterinarians*					X								X	X	X				X	X	X	X	X			46,000	23 to 34	Above average because growth in number of pets and increase in veterinary research.

MEDICAL TECHNOLOGIST, TECHNICIAN, AND ASSISTANT OCCUPATIONS

	Occupation	1	2	3	4	5	6	7	8	9	10	11	12	13	14	15	16	17	18	19	20	21	22	23	24	25	Est. Emp. 1990	Range of Change (hundreds) 1990-2000	Employment Prospects
IB	Electro-cardiograph technicians	X	T			X				X	X			X		X							X	X			18,000	27 to 30	Slower than average growth expected, due to hospital efforts to cut staff costs.

The Career Finder 97

MEDICAL TECHNOLOGIST, TECHNICIAN, AND ASSISTANT OCCUPATIONS

TYPE OF WORK AND CO-WORKERS	OCCUPATION	1 High School diploma	2 Technical school or apprenticeship	3 Junior college	4 College degree	5 Jobs widely scattered	6 Jobs concentrated in locations	7 Work with things	8 Work with ideas	9 Help people	10 Work with people	11 Able to see physical results of work	12 Opportunity for self-expression	13 Work as part of a team	14 Work independently	15 Work closely supervised	16 Direct activity of others	17 Generally confined to work area	18 Overtime or shift work required	19 Outdoors	20 High level of responsibility	21 Requires physical stamina	22 Work with detail	23 Repetitious work	24 Motivate others	25 Competitive	ESTIMATED EMPLOYMENT – 1990	RANGE OF POSSIBLE CHANGE IN EMPLOYMENT (HUNDREDS) 1990-2000	EMPLOYMENT PROSPECTS
IB	Electroencephalographic technologists and technicians*	X	T			X				X	X			X		X		X					X				6,400	29 to 31	Employment expected to grow much faster than average due to use of EEG's in surgery and in diagnosing and monitoring patients with brain disease. Best job prospects for registered technologists and those with formal training.
IB	Medical laboratory workers*	X	2	2	2		X				X	X		X		X			X		X		X				242,000	31 to 35	Average growth expected.
DS	Medical records technicians and clerks	X	2	2		X					X	X				X		X					X	X			47,000	46	Employment expected to grow faster than average due to increased paperwork in hospitals and other health facilities. Job prospects for graduates of approved programs will be excellent.
IB	Optometric assistants	X								X	X			X		X		X					X				18,000	33	Above average due to greater demand for eye care services. Job opportunities for persons who have completed a formal training program should be excellent.
IB	Radiologic (X-ray) technologists*	X	2				X			X	X			X		X		X	X		X		X				132,000	31 to 35	Above average as X-ray equipment is increasingly used to diagnose and treat diseases. Employment prospects generally favorable, but applicants in some areas may face competition.
SI	Respiratory therapy workers	X	2	2		X				X	X			X		X		X	X				X				56,000	12 to 15	Much faster than average due to new applications of respiratory therapy in treating diseases.

98 *How to Choose the Right Career*

			1	2	3	4	5	6	7	8	9	10	11	12	13	14	15	16	17	18	19	20	21	22	23	24	25	ESTIMATED EMPLOYMENT – 1990	RANGE OF POSSIBLE CHANGE IN EMPLOYMENT (HUNDREDS) 1990-2000	EMPLOYMENT PROSPECTS

Column key (1–25): High School diploma; Technical school or apprenticeship; Junior college; College degree; Jobs concentrated in locations; Jobs widely scattered; Work with things; Work with ideas; Help people; Work with people; Able to see physical results of work; Opportunity for self-expression; Work as part of a team; Work independently; Work closely supervised; Direct activity of others; Generally confined to work area; Overtime or shift work required; Outdoors; High level of responsibility; Requires physical stamina; Work with detail; Repetitious work; Motivate others; Competitive

NURSING OCCUPATIONS

	OCCUPATION	1	2	3	4	5	6	7	8	9	10	11	12	13	14	15	16	17	18	19	20	21	22	23	24	25	Est. Empl. 1990	Range 1990-2000	Employment Prospects
SC	Registered nurses*	X	4	4	4	X				X	X	X	X	X	X	X	X	X	X		X	X	X				1,577,000	39 to 44	Employment expected to grow faster than average. Favorable job prospects expected in rural and big city hospitals. Competition may exist in suburban hospitals and in areas with many training facilities.
SC	Licensed practical nurses*	T				X				X	X	X	X	X	X	X	X	X	X			X	X				626,000	28 to 34	Employment expected to grow faster than average as population increases and demand for health care rises. Job prospects are very good.

THERAPY AND REHABILITATION OCCUPATIONS

	OCCUPATION	1	2	3	4	5	6	7	8	9	10	11	12	13	14	15	16	17	18	19	20	21	22	23	24	25	Est. Empl. 1990	Range 1990-2000	Employment Prospects
SB	Occupational therapists				X	X				X	X	X	X	X		X	X				X		X				33,000	22 to 34	Well above average due to public interest in rehabilitation of disabled persons and growth of established occupational therapy programs.
SB	Occupational therapy assistants		2	2		X				X	X	X	X	X	X	X	X				X						39,000	17 to 24	Faster than average due to increased need for assistants in health care institutions. Opportunities should be very good for graduates of approved programs.
SI	Physical therapists				X	X				X	X	X	X	X	X	X	X						X				68,000	34 to 39	Employment expected to grow much faster than average because of increased public concern for rehabilitation services. Job prospects expected to be excellent.

The Career Finder

	OCCUPATION	High School diploma	Technical school or apprenticeship	Junior college	College degree	Jobs widely scattered	Jobs concentrated in locations	Work with things	Work with ideas	Help people	Work with people	Able to see physical results of work	Opportunity for self-expression	Work as part of a team	Work independently	Work closely supervised	Direct activity of others	Generally confined to work area	Outdoors	Overtime or shift work required	High level of responsibility	Requires physical stamina	Work with detail	Repetitious work	Motivate others	Competitive	ESTIMATED EMPLOYMENT – 1990	RANGE OF POSSIBLE CHANGE IN EMPLOYMENT (HUNDREDS) 1990-2000	EMPLOYMENT PROSPECTS
		1	2	3	4	5	6	7	8	9	10	11	12	13	14	15	16	17	18	19	20	21	22	23	24	25			

THERAPY AND REHABILITATION OCCUPATIONS

SB	Physical therapist assistants and aides		2	2		X			X		X	X	X		X		X					X					11,500	52	Above average due to expanding physical therapy services. Opportunities for graduates of approved programs should be excellent.
SC	Speech pathologists and audiologists				+	X			X	X	X	X	X		X		X					X		X			53,000	41 to 47	Employment expected to increase faster than average due to growing public concern over speech and hearing disorders. Persons with only a bachelor's degree will face keen competition for jobs.

OTHER HEALTH OCCUPATIONS

SI	Dietitians				+	X			X	X					X		X					X		X			40,000	31 to 40	Employment expected to grow faster than average in response to increasing concern for proper nutrition and food management. Favorable full- and part-time opportunities for those having a bachelor's degree in foods and nutrition or institution management and the necessary clinical experience.
PD	Health service administrators				+	X					X				X		X			X		X		X	X	X	177,000	31 to 35	Well above average as quantity of patient services increases and health services management becomes more complex.
IP	Pharmacists				+	X		X		X				X			X			X		X		X	X		162,000	11 to 13	Employment expected to grow as fast as average due to aging of the population and increasing use of pharmacists in health care institutions. Employment prospects generally favorable, but keen competition is expected in some areas.

100 *How to Choose the Right Career*

	OCCUPATION	Technical school or apprenticeship	Junior college	College degree	Jobs widely scattered	Jobs concentrated in locations	Work with things	Work with ideas	Help people	Work with people	Able to see physical results of work	Opportunity for self-expression	Work as part of a team	Work independently	Work closely supervised	Direct activity of others	Generally confined to work area	Overtime or shift work required	Outdoors	High level of responsibility	Requires physical stamina	Work with detail	Repetitious work	Motivate others	Competitive	ESTIMATED EMPLOYMENT – 1990	RANGE OF POSSIBLE CHANGE IN EMPLOYMENT (HUNDREDS) 1990-2000	EMPLOYMENT PROSPECTS
		1	2	3	4	5	6	7	8	9	10	11	12	13	14	15	16	17	18	19	20	21	22	23	24	25		

SOCIAL SCIENTISTS

ID	Anthropologists				+	X		X			X		X	X									X			7,100	12 to 15	Most new jobs will be in nonacademic areas. Even persons with Ph.D's can expect keen competition for jobs.
ID	Economists				+	X		X			X		X	X									X			39,500	22 to 27	Master's and Ph.D. degree holders may face keen competition for college and university positions but can expect good opportunities in nonacademic areas. Persons with bachelor's degrees likely to face keen competition.

ART, DESIGN AND COMMUNICATION OCCUPATIONS

PERFORMING ARTISTS

CB	Actors	T				X		X		X		X	X			X					X	X		X	X	41,000	21 to 27	Faster than average growth but overcrowding in this field will persist. Part-time and seasonal employment common.
CB	Dancers	T				X		X		X		X	X			X					X	X		X	X	6,400	17 to 21	Keen competition, most openings being replacements. Teaching offers the best opportunities.
CB	Musicians	T			X			X		X		X	X	X										X	X	229,000	17 to 21	Slower than average growth, and competition will be keen.
CB	Singers	T						X		X		X	X	X									X	X	X	19,000	11 to 19	Employment expected to grow more slowly than average. Applicants likely to face keen competition for jobs.

The Career Finder

DESIGN OCCUPATIONS

	OCCUPATION	TYPE OF WORK AND CO-WORKERS: 1 Jobs widely scattered, 2 Jobs concentrated in locations, 3 Work with things, 4 Work with ideas, 5 Help people, 6 Work with people, 7 Able to see physical results of work, 8 Opportunity for self-expression, 9 Work as part of a team, 10 Work independently, 11 Work closely supervised, 12 Direct activity of others, 13 Generally confined to work area, 14 Overtime or shift work required, 15 Outdoors, 16 High level of responsibility, 17 Requires physical stamina, 18 Work with detail, 19 Repetitious work, 20 Motivate others, 21 Competitive, 22 High School diploma, 23 Technical school or apprenticeship, 24 Junior college, 25 College degree	ESTIMATED EMPLOYMENT – 1990	RANGE OF POSSIBLE CHANGE IN EMPLOYMENT (HUNDREDS) 1990-2000	EMPLOYMENT PROSPECTS
CI	Architects	1: ; 2: ; 3: T; 4: X; 5: X; 6: ; 7: X; 8: ; 9: ; 10: ; 11: X; 12: X; 13: ; 14: ; 15: X; 16: ; 17: X; 18: ; 19: ; 20: ; 21: X; 22: ; 23: X; 24: ; 25:	86,000	31 to 33	Employment expected to rise faster than average, but competition for jobs likely.
CB	Commercial and graphic artists and designers	1: ; 2: ; 3: X; 4: ; 5: X; 6: ; 7: X; 8: ; 9: ; 10: ; 11: X; 12: X; 13: ; 14: ; 15: X; 16: ; 17: X; 18: ; 19: ; 20: ; 21: ; 22: ; 23: X; 24: ; 25:	164,000	3 to 11	Keen competition expected to continue in field. Those with above average talent and skills will be in demand.
BC	Retail display workers	1: X; 2: ; 3: ; 4: ; 5: ; 6: X; 7: X; 8: X; 9: ; 10: ; 11: X; 12: X; 13: X; 14: ; 15: X; 16: ; 17: ; 18: ; 19: ; 20: ; 21: X; 22: ; 23: X; 24: ; 25:	27,000	13 to 19	Employment expected to grow faster than average because of the popularity of visual merchandising—the use of merchandise to decorate stores. Best prospects for those with artistic talent and some college background.
CB	Floral designers	1: X; 2: ; 3: ; 4: ; 5: X; 6: ; 7: X; 8: X; 9: ; 10: ; 11: X; 12: X; 13: ; 14: ; 15: X; 16: ; 17: X; 18: ; 19: ; 20: ; 21: ; 22: ; 23: X X; 24: ; 25:	57,000	3 to 7	Employment will grow more slowly than average as floral outlets in supermarkets increase and people buy more loose flowers rather than arrangements.
CI	Industrial designers	1: ; 2: X; 3: ; 4: X; 5: ; 6: ; 7: X; 8: ; 9: ; 10: X; 11: X; 12: X; 13: ; 14: ; 15: ; 16: ; 17: ; 18: X; 19: ; 20: ; 21: ; 22: X; 23: ; 24: ; 25:	14,600	1 to 2	Below average as trend away from frequent redesign of household products, automobiles, and industrial equipment continues.
CI	Interior designers	1: ; 2: X; 3: ; 4: X; 5: ; 6: ; 7: X; 8: X; 9: ; 10: X; 11: X; 12: X; 13: ; 14: X; 15: ; 16: ; 17: ; 18: ; 19: ; 20: ; 21: ; 22: X; 23: ; 24: ; 25: X	38,000	7 to 10	Increasing use of design services in business and homes should cause average growth. Competition for jobs likely. Best opportunities for talented college graduates in interior design and graduates of professional interior design schools.

102 How to Choose the Right Career

	OCCUPATION	1 Jobs widely scattered	2 Jobs concentrated in locations	3 Work with things	4 Work with ideas	5 Help people	6 Work with people	7 Able to see physical results of work	8 Opportunity for self-expression	9 Work as part of a team	10 Work independently	11 Work closely supervised	12 Direct activity of others	13 Generally confined to work area	14 Overtime or shift work required	15 Outdoors	16 High level of responsibility	17 Requires physical stamina	18 Work with detail	19 Repetitious work	20 Motivate others	21 Competitive	ESTIMATED EMPLOYMENT – 1990	RANGE OF POSSIBLE CHANGE IN EMPLOYMENT (HUNDREDS) 1990-2000	EMPLOYMENT PROSPECTS
DESIGN OCCUPATIONS																									
CI	Landscape architects		7	7	X	X	X		X				X									X	19,000	27 to 29	Employment expected to grow faster than average due to increases in new construction and city and regional environmental planning. Best job prospects for those with graduate degrees in landscape architecture.
CB	Photographers		7	7	X		X	X	X		X	X		X									105,000	11 to 25	Employment expected to grow about as fast as average. Portrait and commercial photographers likely to face keen competition. Good opportunities in areas such as law enforcement and scientific and medical research photography.
COMMUNICATIONS RELATED OCCUPATIONS																									
CI	Reporters and correspondents				X		X		X				X		X						X		70,000	21 to 30	Employment expected to grow about as fast as average. Best opportunities on newspapers and magazines in small towns and suburbs and for graduates who have specialized in news-editorial studies and completed an internship.
CI	Radio and television announcers and newscasters	X				X						X			X							X	57,000	22 to 35	Employment expected to increase as fast as average as new stations are licensed and as cable television stations do more of their own programming. Keen competition likely for openings, however. Best prospects in small cities.

The Career Finder

COMMUNICATIONS RELATED OCCUPATIONS

Column headers (TYPE OF WORK AND CO-WORKERS):
1. Jobs concentrated in locations
2. Jobs widely scattered
3. Work with things
4. Work with ideas
5. Help people
6. Work with people
7. Able to see physical results of work
8. Opportunity for self-expression
9. Work as part of a team
10. Work independently
11. Work closely supervised
12. Direct activity of others
13. Generally confined to work area
14. Overtime or shift work required
15. Outdoors
16. High level of responsibility
17. Requires physical stamina
18. Work with detail
19. Repetitious work
20. Motivate others
21. Competitive
22. College degree
23. Junior college
24. Technical school or apprenticeship
25. High School diploma

	Occupation	1	2	3	4	5	6	7	8	9	10	11	12	13	14	15	16	17	18	19	20	21	22	23	24	25	Est. Empl. 1990	Range of change 1990-2000	Employment Prospects
IC	Technical writers					X		X	X				X	X				X				X					25,000	26 to 36	Better than average growth. Best opportunities for people with both writing ability and a scientific or technical background.
ID	Geographers				+	X	X	X	X			X		X	X							X					18,000	21 to 25	Average. Best prospects for advanced degree holders in the non-academic market.
ID	Historians				X	X	X	X	X					X	X							X					19,800	1 to 2	Employment expected to decline. Keen competition is anticipated, particularly for academic positions. Best opportunities for Ph.D.'s with a strong background in quantitative research methods.
ID	Political scientists				X	X	X	X	X	X												X					15,800	11 to 13	Employment expected to increase more slowly than average. Keen competition likely, especially for academic positions. Best opportunities for advanced degree holders with training in applied fields such as public administration or public policy.
IS	Psychologists				X	X	X	X	X	X											X				X		104,000	21 to 26	Employment expected to grow as fast as average. Graduates face increasing competition, particularly for academic positions. Best prospects for doctoral degree holders trained in applied areas, such as clinical, counseling, health, and industrial psychology.
IS	Sociologists				X	X	X	X	X	X		X										X					21,000	5 to 6	Below average growth. Best opportunities for Ph.D.'s trained in statistical research. Very competitive below Ph.D. level.

How to Choose the Right Career

SOCIAL SERVICE OCCUPATIONS

COUNSELING

	Occupation	1	2	3	4	5	6	7	8	9	10	11	12	13	14	15	16	17	18	19	20	21	22	23	24	25	Estimated Employment – 1990	Range of Possible Change in Employment (Hundreds) 1990-2000	Employment Prospects
SI	School counselors				+	X				X											X				X		67,000	3 to 7	Little change expected in employment due to sharply declining enrollments in secondary schools.
SD	Employment counselors				+	X				X											X						7,600	4 to 6	Dependent on public funding. Keen competition.
SI	Rehabilitation counselors				+	X				X											X						25,600	5 to 7	Employment growth depends upon government funding for vocational rehabilitation agencies. Some openings are expected with insurance companies and consulting firms.
SI	Clergy				+	X				X							X				X				X		252,500	3	Protestant ministers face competition because of mergers. Reform rabbis and Orthodox clergy will also face competition. Good opportunities for Catholic priests.

Column headings (Type of Work and Co-workers):
1. High School diploma
2. Technical school or apprenticeship
3. Junior college
4. College degree
5. Jobs widely scattered
6. Jobs concentrated in locations
7. Work with things
8. Work with ideas
9. Help people
10. Work with people
11. Able to see physical results of work
12. Opportunity for self-expression
13. Work as part of a team
14. Work independently
15. Work closely supervised
16. Direct activity of others
17. Generally confined to work area
18. Overtime or shift work required
19. Outdoors
20. High level of responsibility
21. Requires physical stamina
22. Work with detail
23. Repetitious work
24. Motivate others
25. Competitive

Footnotes

1. Educational requirements vary by industry or employer.
2. Educational requirements vary according to type of work.
3. Estimate not available.
4. Diploma, baccalaureate, and associate degree programs prepare R.N. candidates for licensure.
5. Teachers only.
6. Decrease in employment is expected to be greater than number of openings.
7. Training programs are available from vocational schools or junior colleges.
8. Range less than one percent.

T / + / A — Specialized or technical training needed. / Educational requirements beyond a bachelor's degree. / Availability of official apprenticeship programs.

* Workers use dangerous equipment or material or work in dangerous surroundings.

** B = Body Workers; D, Data Detail; P, Persuaders; S, Service Workers; C, Creative Artists; I, Investigators.

DEVELOPING A GAME PLAN

Part II

Your Educational and Career Alternatives 13

Listed below are 13 of the most common choices of actions to take after high school. Rank them by numbering them 1 to 13 in their order of attractiveness to you. (1= most attractive, 13= least attractive.)

_____ Community college, either for 1- or 2-year vocational training or a program that allows transfer to a four-year college

_____ Four-year college or university

_____ Full-time work

_____ Military service

_____ Business or technical school

_____ Part-time work/part-time college

_____ Apprenticeship program for a trade

_____ Volunteer organization (usually social or religious service)

_____ Unemployment/postponing any commitment

_____ Marriage/homemaking career

_____ Self-employment/start your own business

_____ Fail to graduate and stay in high school

_____ Stopping off (taking a year off between high school and college or other commitment)

After ranking the options in this list, brainstorm other options you have for your future. The objective of brainstorming is to generate as many ideas about your future as you can. If possible, recruit a friend to help brainstorm with you.

Groundrules of brainstorming

1. Make your list of possibilities as long as possible.

2. Put everything in writing.

3. Allow no rights, wrongs, evaluations, or examinations while you are brainstorming.

4. Allow for bizarre and irrational as well as usual and predictable choices.

5. Do not question, discuss, or defend any possibility—just write it down.

6. Ignore the Acceptable/Unacceptable columns below until you have finished your list.

	Acceptable	Unacceptable
I could . . .		
I could . . .		
I could . . .		
I could . . .		
I could . . .		
I could . . .		
I could . . .		
I could . . .		
I could . . .		
I could . . .		

When you have generated as many ideas as possible, decide whether you like or dislike each idea. Indicate this with a check in the appropriate column.

Possible Training Programs and College Majors 14

In the 1990s, three out of every four jobs will require a one- or two-year specialized certificate or associate degree. Today's employers need to hire skilled, trained workers who have recent, relevant training in their fields.

Every worker should consider it necessary to receive education beyond high school. Opportunities in unskilled occupations have been declining. U.S. census statistics continue to show a relationship between the amount of training after high school and the level of income earned, throughout a person's lifetime.

A two-year program in community college can provide you with training that offers some employment security, a decent income, and a growing future. Two-year training programs are today's bargain in higher education for many people.

The Body Workers   Listed below are samples of courses that prepare workers for physically active and technical jobs, especially work involving tools or machines. The jobs may be in the skilled trades, technical, service, or professional trades.

College Programs
Athletics
Biotechnology
Dance
Forestry
Horticulture
Landscape Architecture
Occupational Therapy

Vocational Schools
Agricultural Power Equipment Operation
Air Conditioning Technology
Aircraft Assembly
Aircraft Field Services
Airline Communications
Appliance Servicing
Automobile Mechanics
Aviation
Aviation Electronics
Baking
Bartending
Body and Fender Repair
Building Construction
Business Machine Servicing
Cargo Supervision
Carpentry
Computer Technology
Dairy Technology
Dental Lab Technology
Diesel Mechanics and Technology
Dispatching
Drafting
Driving or Chauffeuring
Dry Cleaning
Earth Moving Machinery Operation
Electrical Power Technology
Electroplating
Engraving
Fisheries
Flight Training
Floor Covering Installation
Floristry
Forestry Technology
Heating Technology
Horticulture
Landscape Architecture
Laundering
Livestock Procurement
Locksmithing
Marine Engineering
Masonry
Metal Trades
Microwave Technology
Motorcycle Repair
Moving
Navigation Technology
Nursery Management
Painting
Paperhanging
Park and Recreation Work
Photography
Plastering
Plumbing
Polygraph Technology
Power Plant Mechanics
Printing Technology
Radar Technology
Radio, TV Repair
Restaurant Practice
Refrigeration
Sewing Machine Operation
Shipbuilding
Sound Systems Technology
Tailoring
Tiling
Tractor Mechanics
Typesetting
Upholstery
Veterinary Technology

Watchmaking
Water Treatment
Welding
Wildlife Management

Military Training Programs
Air Traffic Control
Asphalt Equipment
   Operation
Audio Specialist
Aviation Electronics
Aviation Machinery
   Operation
Boiler Making
Bricklaying
Butchering
Carpentry
Commissary Work
Cooking
Crane Operation
Crawler Tractor Operation
Cryptography
Disbursing Clerk
Dispatching
Driving
Electronics
Electronics Technology
Equipment Repair
Fire Fighting
Grader Operation
Heating and Cooling
   Technology
Lithography
Maintenance
   Administration
Masonry
Painting
Pipe Fitting
Platemaking
Plumbing
Presswork
Radar
Radio Operation
Sheet-Metal Work
Shoe Repair
Silk-Screen Printing
Storekeeper

Structural Mechanics
Telephone Operation
Textile and Leather Repair
Welding
Woodworking

Apprenticeships
Aircraft Fabrication
Airplane Mechanics
Arboretum Work
Asbestos Work
Auto Mechanics
Boiler Making
Bookbinding
Stationary Engineering
Steam Fitting
Stonemasonry
Textile Technology
Tile Laying
Tool-and-Die Making
Truck Mechanics
Upholstery
Wood Carving

Cooperative Programs
Aerospace Technology
Brewery Work
Bricklaying
Butchery
Cabinetmaking
Candy Making
Canvas Work
Carpentry
Carpet Laying
Cement Masonry
Composition
Cosmetology
Dental Technology
Electrical Technology
Engraving
Ironwork
Jewelry Making
Lathe Making
Leather Work
Lithography
Meat Cutting

Molding
Ophthalmic Technology
Painting
Patternmaking
Photoengraving
Pipe Fitting
Plastering
Platemaking
Plumbing
Presswork
Rigging
Roofing
Sheet-Metal Work

Agriculture
Applied Mechanics
Aviation Maintenance
Building Construction
Carpentry
Ceramics
Chemical Technology
Electronics
Fire Protection
Forestry
Recreation Technology
Welding

The Data Detail   The following courses prepare workers for white-collar jobs involving clerical or numerical tasks.

College Majors
Accounting
Actuarial Science
Appraisal
Business
Business Administration
Business Teacher Education
Computer Programming
Finance
International Business
Real Estate and Urban
    Land Economics

Aviation Administration
Data Processing
Medical Technology
Secretarial Science
Stenography
Cashiering
Claims Adjusting
Computer Operation
Computer Programming
Court Reporting
Tax Preparation
Typing
Word Processing

Vocational Programs
Accountancy
Banking
Bookkeeping
Data Processing
Estimating
Insurance Adjusting
Keypunching
PBX Switchboard
    Operation

Cooperative Programs
Accounting
Administration

Military Training
Bookkeeping
Computer Operation
Court Reporting
Journalism
Legal Services Assisting
Machine Accounting
Medical Records
Personnel
Programming
Stenography

114 *How to Choose the Right Career*

The Persuaders These college majors and vocational programs prepare workers to hold jobs where they persuade people to perform some kind of action.

College Majors	
Communication Arts	Buying
Educational Administration	Credit and Collection
Health Services	Fashion Merchandising
Administration	Food Service
Industrial Relations	Hotel and Motel
International Relations	Management
Law	Insurance Sales
Management	Market Training
Political Science	Medical Office Management
Programming	Merchandising
Public Administration	Real Estate Sales
Retailing	Receptionist
Urban and Regional	Retail Management
Planning	Travel Agent
	Travel Guide

Vocational Schools	*Cooperative Programs*
Advertising	Advertising
Airline Reservations	Fashion Merchandising
Apartment House	Marketing
Management	Retail Management
Auctioneering	Sales Training

The Service Workers The following courses prepare workers to hold jobs where they heal, teach, or help people.

College Majors	*Vocational Schools*
Behavioral Science	Child Care and Guidance
Child Development	Community Organization
Communication Disorders	Cosmetology
Counseling	Dental Assistance
Education	Dietetics
Nursing	Electrical Technology
Occupational Therapy	Family Assistance
Physical Therapy	Flight Attendant Training
Psychology	Hospital Admitting
Social Studies	Work
Social Work	Infant Care
Sociology	Inhalation Therapy

Law Enforcement
Medical Assistance
Medical Records Technology
Optical Dispensing
Paramedic Training
Practical Nursing
Radiation Therapy

Military
Dental Technician Specialist

E.K.G., E.E.G. Specialist
Operating Room Assistant
Physical Therapy Technologist
Prosthetic Appliance Specialist
Psychiatric Technician
Radiation Therapy Technologist
Social Work Assistant
X-ray Operator

The Creative Artists

These courses prepare workers to use words, music, graphics, dance, painting, or other forms of art to express thought or feeling in a creative way.

College Majors
Art
Broadcasting
Classics
Communication Arts
Comparative Literature
Computer Graphics
Computerized Music
Dance
English
Interior Design
Journalism
Languages
Music
Photography
Theater and Drama
TV Production

Vocational Programs
Acting
Advertising Art
Architecture
Bookbinding
Broadcasting
Cartography
Cartooning
Ceramics

Computer Graphics
Costume Design
Creative Writing
Dance
Darkroom Techniques
Drafting
Educational Media Technology
Engraving
Fashion Design
Fashion Illustration
Furniture Design
Interior Design
Journalism
Layout
Package Design
Pantomime
Photography
Playwriting
Radio Announcing
Sculpture
Sign Painting
Silk-Screen Printing
Technical Illustrating
Theater Production
TV Production
Weaving

116   *How to Choose the Right Career*

Military Programs
Communications
Illustrating

Photography
Special Services

The Investigators

These courses prepare workers to investigate how the world is put together. The work usually involves scientific or laboratory work.

College Majors
Anatomy
Anthropology
Astronomy
Astrophysics
Bacteriology
Behavioral Disabilities
Behavioral Science
Biochemistry
Biology
Biomedical Engineering
Biophysics
Chemical Engineering
Chemistry
Dietetics
Earth Science
Electrical Engineering
Electronic Engineering
Endocrinology
Entomology
Forestry
Genetics
Geography
Industrial Engineering
Medical Science
Meteorology
Nuclear Medicine
Neurophysiology
Neurosciences
Oceanography
Pathology
Pharmacy
Physical Therapy
Physiology

Plant Genetics
Quantitative Analysis
Statistics
Zoology

*Vocational Schools and/or
   Technical Institutes*
Aerospace Engineering
Architectural Engineering
Ceramics
Chemical Engineering
Civil Engineering
Industrial Engineering
   Technology
Metallurgical Engineering
Mechanical Engineering
Mineral Engineering
Oceanographic Engineering
Petroleum Engineering
Plastics Engineering
Quality Control
Surveying
Technical Writing
Testing Technology

Military Training
Intelligence Specialist
Radar Technologist
Sonar Specialist
Structural Engineer
Technical Engineer
Weather Observer

Choosing a College 15

Fill in the next few pages if you are seriously considering going to college either right after graduation or at some later date. If you think you *might* consider going to college someday, it's useful to fill them in, too.

The following list includes some of the reasons for choosing a particular college. Rank the five reasons that most influence you. Give a *1* to your strongest reason, a *2* to the next strongest, and so on. Be sure to read all the reasons listed here, and also consider any other factors you think might influence your decision.

_____ Go to the college nearest home.

_____ Go to a college where you know other students.

_____ Go to the college that is recruiting hardest for students.

_____ Go to the college with the most desired program.

_____ Make a systematic survey of the universities and colleges available and select the one most meaningful to you.

_____ Choose the college according to its tuition and living fees.

_____ Go to the college whose admission requirements can be met.

_____ Go to the college you believe will best affect your selection of friends, spouse, religious, political, and career values.

_____ Go to the college which will best qualify you for graduate school.

_____ Go to the college with the most social atmosphere.

_____ Go to the college with an intellectual atmosphere, giving much academic responsibility to students.

_____ Go to the college that is a parent's or other influential person's choice.

_____ Other (explain)_____

Check the appropriate answer to these questions.

	Yes	No
Are you willing to commit yourself to a lengthy, expensive education?		
Do you want to enlarge your intellectual horizons?		
Do you want to develop skills for a specific occupation that requires a college education?		
Do you want to meet people with similar interests?		
Do you want to learn how to learn and how to think clearly?		
Are you willing to give hours each day to study and practice?		

You should probably have three or more "yes" answers if you are ready to benefit from college and make it worth the investment.

Should You Choose a Large School or a Small School?

Check the items below that truly describe your behavior.

_____ Tend to cut class.

_____ Frequently tend to quit what you are doing.

_____ Shun active participation in class and school activities.

_____ Tend to get lost in crowds.

_____ Need encouragement to be involved and productive in many activities.

_____ Shy, tend to socialize with only a few people.

_____ Friendly, frequently greet people and mix well with people.

_____ Will attend class without supervision or the teacher knowing you are there.

_____ Persevere in the path which you choose.

_____ Have a history of active participation in class and school functions.	_____ Have a history of very productive school activity.
_____ Have assumed responsibility and importance in a wide range of school activities.	_____ Would utilize extensive facilities, well-stocked library, etc.

If most of your checks are in the left column, a small school may be best for you. If most of your checks are on the right, then a large school may be best.

An important part of deciding on a college is coming to terms with expenses involved. You will need to know specific costs for tuition, extra fees, room and board, books, transportation to and from school, and personal expenses. You should compare the costs at each of the schools you have considered attending, and weigh these factors with the others when you are choosing the college you will attend.

An excellent source of information about scholarships and financial aid is published each year and is available free. It is *Meeting Your College Costs* and can be ordered from The College Entrance Examination Board, Box 592, Princeton, New Jersey 08540. It gives step-by-step directions for when and where to apply for financial aid.

Other Factors to Consider When Choosing a College

1. Two-year or four-year?
   Do you have a poor high school record? Many two-year community colleges have open admissions policies and programs to help students develop academic skills. Are finances a concern? Again, a community college may be the solution, since for two years you can live at home, attend school for a low tuition, and then complete your training at a more expensive four-year university.

2. Academic difficulty
   To find a college which will be sufficiently stimulating for you, you should evaluate your College Board scores and compare them with your high school grades. The *College Handbook* edited by

Douglas D. Dillenbeck and the *Comparative Guide to American Colleges* by Max Birnbaum and James Cass are especially helpful in matching your abilities with the right school.

3. Location
   Do you want to be in the heart of a large city, or do you do best in a small-town atmosphere? Send for catalogs, visit campuses, and then make an informed choice.

Which College Major Is Best?

In a recent survey, college graduates were asked which college courses they found most useful in their work. The vast majority of graduates surveyed said their education increased their general knowledge and helped them get a good job. Less than one quarter said their training was useful for increasing their leadership abilities or in helping them select career goals.

When asked which courses they would recommend to college students, the graduates most frequently suggested courses in business administration, English, and psychology. Other highly recommended courses were economics, accounting, and mathematics. Regardless of their occupations, graduates stressed the need for skills in communication—writing and speaking—administration, and working with people.

If you are planning to enter college, you may wish to select a major immediately. If so, you may already have an idea of your major interest. Whether or not you have already made up your mind about your major, you should discuss it with people who are already in the field that interests you, with a high school guidance counselor, and the admissions and major department counselors at the college. This can be done by correspondence and/or in person. Your friends and family may provide insight, too, in career areas they know, and in helping you to analyze your own special talents and problem areas. If family sessions about your choice become too emotional, it sometimes is a great help to have present a third, outside party, like the high school career counselor, or a teacher or family friend who has information or experience to bring to the discussion.

Colleges usually allow a year or two of attendance before requiring a student to select a major. If you do not already know what you want your major to be, you will have time to think about it while you learn about various majors. The broad curriculum that is usually required in the freshman year should aid your decision making by exposing you to many subjects.

Should You Join the Military?

Military service provides an alternative to many high school graduates, and may also provide a vehicle for later education. Think over the questions listed below, for clues to whether or not you would be happy in the military. Write in yes or no.

_____ Do you want to explore life before deciding on long-range plans?

_____ Do you want to learn a technical skill or earn a college degree with no financial expense?

_____ Do you want to live away from home and meet many new people?

_____ Do you want to begin a career right away that can lead to an early, well-paying retirement?

_____ Do you want adequate salary immediately plus housing, meals, 30-day vacation, and PX privileges?

_____ Do you want to travel?

_____ Do you want to be eligible for veteran's benefits like education, counseling, preferred mortgage rates, life insurance?

_____ Can you accept that in the event of war you will risk physical injury and death for yourself and inflicting injury or death on others?

_____ Can you live a regimented life-style with a set time to get up, eat, and go to bed?

_____ Can you accept authoritarian leadership where "an order is an order"?

_____ Can you live in barracks with almost no privacy?

_____ Can you live in a situation where it is almost impossible to resign, as you can in private employment?

_____ Would it be good to put yourself in a situation where you will be forced to stay with the job long enough to learn its rewards and successes?

If you answer "yes" to most of these questions, military service may provide a good alternative for you. You may want to talk to friends who have enlisted, as well as representatives of the military services in your area.

Choosing a Vocational School 16

Hands-on training with actual equipment used in such fields as beauty culture, auto mechanics, and computer technology is provided by vocational schools. Vocational schools usually provide placement services as well.

Vocational schools are achievement-oriented; they contract with you to teach you the minimum skills you will need to get a job in a given field. About 40 percent of each day in the vocational school is spent in job-like situations; the rest is spent in classes.

The questions below will help you decide whether vocational school is right for you:

_____ Would you like to learn things that help you do something concrete and productive on your job?

_____ Do you want to complete your training in a relatively short period of time?

Consumer's Guide to Vocational Schools

The following are some questions that should be thought over when shopping for the best vocational school. Find out the answers and consider them carefully.

What are my objectives?

How do students at the school rate their courses?

Who are the teachers? (Teachers at private schools sometimes have more practical experience than teachers at community college vocational programs.)

Do I have the necessary prerequisites? (If you are deficient in high school math, science, or some other requirement, find out how you can fulfill that requirement.)

Ask yourself, "What will happen to me if I enroll in this school?" "What will this course lead to?"

What kinds of students will be in class with you?

What will be the total cost to complete the training? (Include expenses as well as tuition.) Ask the school to supply a *written statement* of what your total costs would be.

What proportion of students have completed their training at this institution? Last year? The year before?

How much money do graduates make on their jobs after training?

How do employers who have hired graduates of the school evaluate the school?

Is the school listed with the Better Business Bureau, the State Department of Public Instruction, or an accrediting agency? (If the school is not accredited, be very careful in evaluating it.)

Factors to look for when studying a vocational school catalog

Will placement assistance, housing assistance, or parking cost extra? (Placement services should be provided without additional charge.)

Are the endorsements and testimonials for the school current, relevant, and truthful?

Do the school's publicity photos and illustrations create any false impressions?

Does the equipment in the photographs actually belong to the school?

Does the catalog have a recent date?

Sources for finding vocational schools

Yellow Pages under "Schools"

Consumer Advice Office of your state. It publishes a *Directory of Approved Private Trade and Technical Schools.*

Consider an Apprenticeship 17

Apprenticeship is a training system, based on written agreement, by which a worker learns a skilled craft or trade. Apprenticeship programs are conducted by the voluntary cooperation of labor unions, management, schools, and government. They are usually conducted wholly on the job.

An apprenticeship program may be right for you if you can answer "yes" to most of the following questions.

- Do you enjoy working with your hands, and are you good at it?
- Are you patient enough to work with precision?
- Do you definitely want to learn a skilled trade that is taught through an apprenticeship?
- Are you willing to invest the next two to five years learning a trade?

- Can you afford to live on a low wage scale while learning?
- Do you value the security and regular salary increases that go with the trade after you complete an apprenticeship?
- Are you willing to settle down, make a choice, and be committed to it?
- Are you between 18 and 30 years of age and in good physical health?
- Can you pass the entrance test? State employment services or apprenticeship information centers, ALF-CIO, The Urban League, and Worker's Defense League, among others, have programs that prepare people for the entrance exams.

For information about apprenticeships, write to:
U.S. Department of Apprenticeship and Training
Department of Labor
Washington, DC 20202

More information about opportunity in your area is available from the nearest regional office. These offices, along with the states they serve are as follows:

Region I
(CT, ME, MA, NH, RI, VT)
Room 1703-A
John F. Kennedy Federal Building
Government Center
Boston, MA 02203

Region II
(NY, NJ, Puerto Rico, Virgin Islands)
201 Varick Street
New York, NY 10001

Region III
(DE, MD, PA, VA, WV)
Gateway Building, Room 13240
3535 Market Street
Philadelphia, PA 19104

Region IV
(AL, FL, GA, KY, MS, NC, SC, TN)
1371 Peachtree Street, NE
Atlanta, GA 30367

Region V
(IL, IN, MI, MN, OH, WI)
Federal Building, Room 701
230 S. Dearborn Street
Chicago, IL 60604

Region VI
(AR, LA, NM, OK, TX)
525 Griffin Street, Room 858
Dallas, TX 75202

Region VII
(IA, KS, MO, NE)
Federal Office Building, Room 1100
911 Walnut Street
Kansas City, MO 64106

Region VIII
(CO, MT, ND, SD, UT, WY)
U.S. Custom House, Room 476
471-19th Street
Denver, CO 80202

Region IX
(AZ, CA, HI, NV, Trust Territories)
211 Main Street, Room 343
San Francisco, CA 94105

Region X
(AK, ID, WA, OR)
Federal Office Building, Room 8018
909 First Avenue
Seattle, WA 98174

The state offices are:

Alabama
2nd Avenue, N., Suite 102-2017
Berry Building
Birmingham, 35203

Alaska
Room E-512
Federal Building & Courthouse, Box 37
701 C Street
Anchorage, 99513

Arizona
3221 N. 16th Street, Suite 302
Phoenix, 85016

Arkansas
Federal Building, Room 3014
700 W. Capitol Street
Little Rock, 72201

California
Division of Apprenticeship Standards
Department of Industrial Relations
211 Main Street
San Francisco, 94105

Colorado
Apprenticeship Council
U.S. Custom House
721-19th Street, Room 480
Denver, 80202

Connecticut
Apprenticeship Training Division
Labor Department
Federal Building, Room 367
135 High Street
Hartford, 06103

Delaware
State Apprenticeship and Training Council
Department of Labor and Industry
Lock Box 36, Federal Building
844 King Street
Wilmington, 19801

District of Columbia
D.C. Apprenticeship Council
555 Pennsylvania Avenue, NW, Room 307
Washington, DC 20201

Florida
Bureau of Apprenticeship
Division of Labor
State of Florida Department of Commerce
Hobbs Federal Building
227 N. Bronough Street
Tallahassee, 32301

Georgia
Apprenticeship Division, Room 203
1371 Peachtree Street, NE
Atlanta, 30367

Hawaii
Apprenticeship Division
Department of Labor and Industrial Relations
300 Ala Moana Boulevard, Room 5113
Honolulu, 96850

Kansas
Apprenticeship Training Division
Federal Building, Room 370
444 S.E. Quincy Street
Topeka, 66683

Kentucky
Kentucky State Apprenticeship
  Council
Federal Building, Room 554-C
600 Federal Place
Louisville, 40202

Louisiana
Division of Apprenticeship
F. Edward Herbert Building, Room
  925
600 S. Maestri Street
New Orleans, 70130

Maine
Maine Apprenticeship Council
Federal Building, Room 101-B
P.O. Box 917
68 Sewall Street
Augusta, 04330

Maryland
Maryland Apprenticeship and
  Training Council
Charles Center—Federal Building,
  Room 1028
31 Hopkins Plaza
Baltimore, 21201

Massachusetts
Division of Apprenticeship Training
JFK Federal Building, Room E-432
Government Center
Boston, 02203

Minnesota
Division of Voluntary
  Apprenticeship
Federal Building, Room 134
316 Robert Street
St. Paul, 55101

Montana
Montana Apprenticeship Council
Federal Office Building
Room 394-Drawer # 10055
301 South Park Avenue.
Helena, 59626-0055

Nevada
Nevada Apprenticeship Council
Post Office Building, Room 311
P.O. Box 1987
301 East Stewart Avenue
Las Vegas, 89101

New Hampshire
New Hampshire Apprenticeship
  Council
Federal Building, Room 311
55 Pleasant Street
Concord, 03301

New Mexico
New Mexico Apprenticeship Council
Western Bank Building, Room 1705
505 Marquette, NW
Albuquerque, 87102

New York
Bureau of Apprenticeship Training
Federal Building, Room 810
North Pearl & Clinton Avenues
Albany, 12201

North Carolina
Division of Apprenticeship Training
Federal Building, Room 376
310 New Bern Avenue
Raleigh, 27601

Ohio
Ohio State Apprenticeship Training
Room 605
200 North High Street
Columbus, 43215

Oregon
Apprenticeship and Training
  Division
Federal Building, Room 526
1220 SW 3rd Avenue
Portland, 97204

Pennsylvania
Pennsylvania Apprenticeship and
  Training Council
Federal Building, Room 773
228 Walnut Street
Harrisburg, 17108

Puerto Rico
Apprenticeship Division,
  Department of Labor
414 Barbosa Avenue
Hato Rey, 00917

Rhode Island
Rhode Island Apprenticeship Council
100 Hartford Avenue
Federal Building
Providence, 02909

Utah
Utah State Apprenticeship Council
Room 1051
1745 W. 1700 Street
Salt Lake City, 84104

Vermont
Vermont Apprenticeship Council
96 College Street, Suite 103
State Office Building
Burlington Square
Burlington, 05401

Virginia
Division of Apprenticeship Training
400 N. 8th Street, Room 10-020
Richmond, 23240

Virgin Islands
Division of Apprenticeship and
  Training
Department of Labor
Christiansted, St. Croix 00820

Washington
Apprenticeship Division
Federal Building, Room B-102
909 First Avenue
Seattle, 98174

Wisconsin
Division of Apprenticeship and
  Training
Federal Center, Room 303
212 East Washington Street
Madison, 53703

Consider Correspondence Schools, Cooperative Programs, and On-the-Job Training | 18

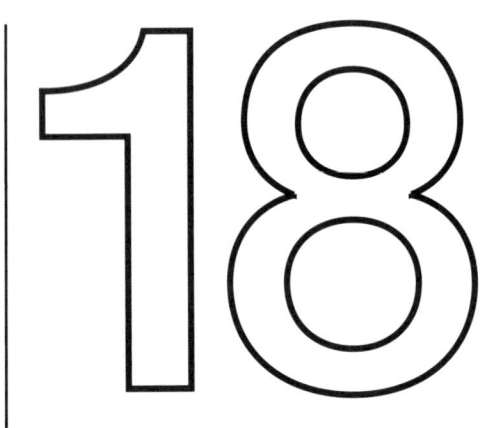

Correspondence and Television Schools

There are advantages and disadvantages to study through correspondence schools. Correspondence schools offer courses that can be completed at home. You receive textbooks, study guides, assignments, and tests through the mail. Some schools use cassette tapes as well. You complete an assignment on your own and mail it to the school, where it is graded and returned.

A correspondence school may be right for you if you answer "yes" to most of these questions:

_____ Are you self-disciplined enough to adhere to a study schedule that is entirely voluntary?

_____ Are you a good finisher as well as beginner? (Many people begin correspondence courses, but few complete them.)

_____ Are you good at working alone, proceeding at your own pace?

_____ Are you highly motivated and self-disciplined?

_____ Must you work while you complete your education?

_____ Do you live where classroom courses are unavailable?

The National Home Study Council is the recognized accrediting agency for correspondence schools. Beware of any school not accredited by the council, since there have been instances of correspondence schools failing to live up to acceptable standards in business and educational practices.

Some colleges and universities offer courses by correspondence. Usually the student can do the studying and writing by correspondence, and the college gives a final exam at the college or a branch. Sometimes, however, it's possible to set up a procedure for final exams in your own community if you are a great distance from the school.

Correspondence courses in combination with television classes on regular commercial or educational television channels are another convenient alternative. They may save you time and money for some of your college courses, or they may provide opportunities for review or monitoring of a course just as a viewer, if you do not need the college credits.

Cooperative Programs

Cooperative programs are programs in which the student attends classes part of the time and works at a related job part time. There are cooperative programs leading to bachelor's degrees as well as cooperative vocational programs. Your study in the classroom is related to the kind of work you do on your job.

A cooperative program may be best for you if you are willing to devote a period of time to part-time work and part-time learning.

For a complete list of programs and schools that offer cooperative programs, consult the *Directory of Cooperative Education,* found in the reference section of most libraries.

On-the-Job Training Programs

Many people choose to go to work full time, directly from high school. There are many on-the-job training programs in which these people can get training. J.T.P.A. (Job Training Partnership Act) programs in your area may be able to help you locate an on-the-job, or OTJ, training program.

Do you want to complete your training in a week to a few months? Do you want to earn full pay while you learn? Are you interested in working for a giant corporation like IBM, Sperry Rand, AT&T, or a city hospital, police, or fire department? All of these employers provide training programs for many positions. Other organizations have training programs as well.

Predict the Results 19

The ability to look ahead is an asset to the decision maker, who must foresee what will happen if certain choices are made. Try to foresee what might happen if you did each of the following. Write your prediction next to each action.

What would be the result if you . . .	Likely results in five years
Got married next year	
Joined the Coast Guard	
Went away to college	

Got a job in a factory	
Travelled abroad for a year	

List here some other possible actions you could take. Predict their results. At left, write whether the action is very, moderately, or slightly important.

Importance	Possible action	Likely result in five years

Overcome Your Barriers 20

Risk: the possibility of suffering harm or loss; danger.

One of the most common barriers to good decision making is fear of *risk*. Every choice involves risk. The repercussions of a decision can be good, or they can cause pain. Even a typical day has some risks. Consider what these people have to decide:

Veronica: Whether to walk to school in the rain or use her lunch money for bus fare.

José: Whether to show up at work without his hard hat or stay away until tomorrow.

Jackie: Whether to go back to school for her G.E.D. or stay with her waitress job for now.

What are some risks each of these people face?

Veronica: _____

José: _____

Jackie: _____

What happens if they decide not to take any risks at all?

_____

_____

_____

Take a Risk Today

Risk taking begins with the small. What is a decision that you have made and acted on today?

_____

What happened to you because of that decision and action?

Bad things that happened (losses) _____

_____

Good things that happened (gains) _____

_____

The more you learn to move right along, do what you really want to do, and take the risks that go with your decisions, the more confident and active you will become. You will find that once you are an experienced risk-taker you cannot go back. You cannot unlearn your habit of risk taking. You cannot unlearn your confidence. Risk taking causes failure but also success. With success comes confidence, responsibility, power, and rewards.

The "I Can'ts"

Besides fear of risk, another barrier to good decision making is the "I can'ts." Your "I can'ts" are internal messages you give yourself regarding your aptitudes, personality, personal attitudes, or prejudices. People frequently express their "I can'ts" by explaining, "I can't do that. That's just the way I am!"

What are some of your "I can'ts?"

I can't _____

I can't _____

I can't _____

I can't _____

I can't _____

Are any of your "I can'ts" preventing you from pursuing a desirable goal? What are some of your "I can'ts" that you would like to change? Go ahead and write them down as "I cans!"

I can (and I will) _____

I can (and I will) _____

I can (and I will) _____

The "You Can'ts" (Other People's Expectations)

Other people's expectations can severely limit your options—if you let them! A young man announces that he would rather go to vocational school than college; a girl announces her intention to become a carpenter. Both deviate from what people expect of them.

His parents say, "You can't do that! All your brothers went to college. You should too."

Her parents say, "You don't want a man's job! Why don't you go into nursing or interior decorating?"

Comments like these can be powerful barriers to achieving goals.

What are some of your "you can'ts?"

Some "You can'ts" involve race or sex discrimination, financial need, educational opportunities, the job market, attitudes of society, family responsibilities, and educational background.

List here three possible goals you could decide on. Then evaluate how your parent and your best friend would feel about each goal.

_____   _____ parent

                                                  _____ friend

_____   _____ parent

                                                  _____ friend

_____   _____ parent

                                                  _____ friend

Summarize Your Information 21

When you have gathered and assembled your information, it is time to act. Everyone has fears and worries that form barriers to action. To live in fear is to become immobilized, incapable of action.

The activities in this book all imply possible action. Think of two possible career actions you could now take. Then think of all the fears and worries you have about why these two actions would make you unhappy. List these reasons under Barriers to Action. Then try to think of actions—concrete moves—you can make to relieve your fears and worries.

(Sample)
Attractive Career Action: Take course in word processing

	Barriers to Action	**Breaking the Barriers to Action**
	1. Long inconvenient bus ride	1. Get in a car pool
	2. Ties up 2 nights a week	2. Plan chores to accomplish more the other nights at home

Breakthrough Plans Attractive Career Action: _____

Barriers to Action	Breaking the Barriers to Action
1. _____	1. _____
2. _____	2. _____

Attractive Career Action: _____

Barriers to Action	Breaking the Barriers to Action
1. _____	1. _____
2. _____	2. _____

Summarize Your Information 143

Decision Wrap-Up   What have you decided to do while working with this book? Try to form some long-range and immediate goals using a "so that" phrase:

In five years, I will have _____

so that _____

In one year, I will have _____

so that _____

In six months, I will have _____

so that _____

Next week, I will have _____

so that _____

Today, I will have _____

so that _____

MARKETING YOURSELF

Part III

A Consumer's Guide to Job Search Strategies 22

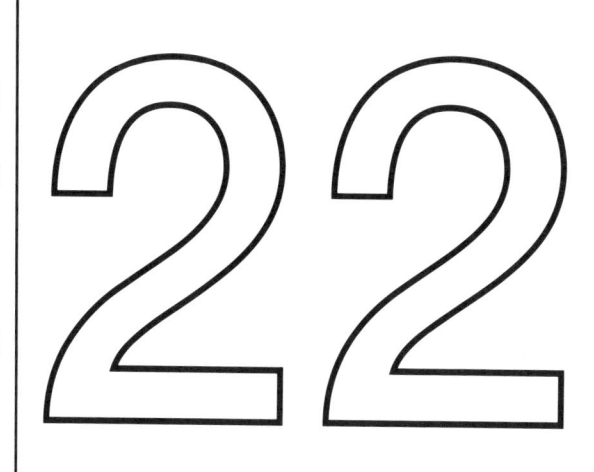

The employment game is a game of numbers. It will help you to recognize that a large number of people will vie against you for the good positions. Other big numbers of the employment game are: the hours you will need to devote to a successful job search; the number of resumes, letters, and phone calls you will need to aim at employers; the number of interviews you will need to have a choice between job offers. This book's quotient for winning the employment game looks like this:

If you want:	Multiply by	And plan on:
2 job offers	5	10 interviews
10 interviews	5	50 letters, resumes, and phone calls
50 contacts	3	150 hours spent on your job search

The trickiest part of the employment game is finding leads that will result in job offers. The three best methods are

1. Applying directly to employers
2. Asking friends for job leads
3. Consulting newspaper want ads

In times when the economy has slowed down, you may have to work twice as hard to get the job leads. The U.S. Department of Labor surveyed ten million job seekers about how they set up interviews that resulted in job offers. The most effective method for nearly every occupation was applying directly to the employer. Answering newspaper ads came in second. Private employment agencies, unions, and tips from friends also helped people win the employment game. Seventy-five percent of the job hunters using any one of these methods remained unemployed, so the key to a successful job search will be to combine a variety of job search methods.

Networking Networking means using your contacts to win the employment game.

Case Study:

Michelle has just graduated from college and wants to start a career in public relations. Her parents, family, and college friends have no connections and offer no help. But one of Michelle's roommates, Marie Sims, has a father who owns his own public relations agency. Michelle asks Marie to see if her father will talk with her.

Mr. Sims agrees to talk with Michelle, making it clear that he has no job to offer her. He tells her the name of the one agency in town willing to hire inexperienced people. Michelle contacts the agency and, with some good interviewing techniques, lands her job.

Job Analysis:

Without using her contacts, Michelle might never have found her job. Unconsciously, she stumbled on to one of the best resources for finding a job: networking.

Over 90 percent of all jobs are never advertised formally. They are filled through word of mouth. People hear that a position is open and apply directly to the employer. Agencies and newspaper ads are not needed to fill the vacancy. Studies show that people who get jobs in this manner stay the longest and get the highest raises.

The chart on the next page will help you to apply the principles of networking. It provides space to write down the names of ten people you know who can be of help to you in locating job possibilities. If each of these people can tell you of other people who are good potential contacts, you will have a list of 100 possible contacts.

Preliminary List of Contacts for Networking

My Friends, Relatives, and Acquaintances	Their Friends, Relatives, and Acquaintances Who May Be Helpful Contacts
1. _____	_____
2. _____	_____
3. _____	_____
4. _____	_____
5. _____	_____
6. _____	_____
7. _____	_____
8. _____	_____
9. _____	_____
10. _____	_____

Developing Your List for Networking

- -

Name: _____

Address: _____

Phone: _____

How could this person assist me? _____

_____

How should I approach her/him? _____

_____

- -

Name: _____

Address: _____

Phone: _____

How could this person assist me? _____

_____

How should I approach her/him? _____

_____

- -

Name: _____

Address: _____

Phone: _____

How could this person assist me? _____

_____

How should I approach her/him? _____

_____

Newspaper Ads

Case study

Tony beats the neighborhood dogs in retrieving his Sunday *Chicago Tribune* off the drive within seconds of its delivery. Moments later, he is engrossed in the "Mid-America Job Guide," which along with the help-wanted ads in New York and Los Angeles papers, is one of the thickest lists of jobs available. The paper lists thousands of job openings in alphabetical order. Surely Tony ought to land one of them. Tony looks over the paper and finds one which sounds intriguing. The ad asks that resumes be sent to a post office box.

Tony sends his resume to the P.O. box and receives a call, not from an employer, but from a local employment agency. The job Tony was interested in didn't exist at all; the ad was placed to get clients for the agency.

Tony tries again the following Sunday. One ad gives a telephone number. Tony phones the company. A crisp, professional voice fires dozens of questions. Tony feels he is responding fine, but then he is asked, "Do you own your own car?" Tony says no. The employer replies that this job requires a personal automobile and hangs up. Tony has been screened out before even having an interview.

Another ad asks for a resume, which Tony promptly mails out. Tony's letter arrives with a batch of 300 other responses to the ad and is given a 15-second reading. A few weeks later he receives a form letter that his was only one of many fine applications received and that his resume will be kept on file.

Tony has dead-ended on three job leads. He might have fared better if he had been familiar with a strategy for successfully using help-wanted ads.

Timing your response

If an advertisement appears in a large Sunday paper such as the *New York Times* or *Chicago Tribune,* send a letter to arrive near the end of the week following the ad. Mail received earlier in the week is more likely to get lost in the shuffle. There may be 300 responses to an ad where the address of the employer is given and the returns will probably come in like this:

SUNDAY—(day the ad appears)

MONDAY—5 resumes received

TUESDAY—55 resumes received

WEDNESDAY—105 resumes received

THURSDAY—60 resumes received

FRIDAY—20 resumes received

LATER—55 resumes received

People don't usually buy the first pair of shoes they try on, nor do they usually hire the first person they interview. You should not be afraid to answer ads that appeared a week or two earlier. The position might not yet be filled, or the person hired for the job might not have worked out.

Selecting ads to answer

Employers rarely find people who meet all the criteria asked for in the advertisement. If you feel you could handle a job, answer the ad even if you don't have the education or industry experience required.

Answering blind ads

About 75 percent of all help-wanted ads are *blind ads.* This means that the employer is not identified. Usually the ad asks you to write to a box number. Employers place blind ads to avoid responding to all applicants, to maintain secrecy with other employees or competitors, or to receive more responses than they would if their identity were known. Employment agencies run such ads to gain clients.

You may have an advantage if you can identify the employer placing the ad and apply directly without referring to the ad. One way to "crack" the identity of the ad is to apply directly to all companies who fit the company's description. For example, if the ad states that the company is an electronics firm in southern Texas, send a letter and resume to all electronics firms in the area.

Responding to ads by telephone

Avoid answering any questions over the telephone. Interviewers cannot meet with everyone, so they try to do some preliminary weeding of job candidates over the telephone.

If the ad gives a phone number, use it only to set up an appointment. Say something like "I'm at work and can't talk now. Could I come in for an interview?" Once the employer sees your potential, he or she may overlook a job requirement or consider you for another job opening.

Salary information Do not give any salary information, even when asked to do so. Even if you appear to be the right person for the job, a too-high or too-low salary figure might disqualify you. Try to answer questions about salary with a question, such as "What is the salary range you have in mind?"

Answering the following questions should help you clarify what an ad is saying and whether you want the job.

Job Advertised: _____

Employer: _____

Publication: _____ Date: _____

1. What requirements and personal qualities should the applicant have?

_____

_____

2. Does the job require "experience"? Have you had non-paid or educational work that could substitute for job experience?

_____

_____

3. Is any information missing? (Location, salary, duties, or employer's name)

_____

_____

If you cannot answer all of these questions from the ad, call the company or use the library to get further information.

4. What are the employer's products or services?

5. Is the name of the person who will do the interviewing mentioned? Is this name real? (Some names are codes to help the company know where you learned about the job.) What is the interviewer's name?

6. What would be your duties in this position?

7. What are the current needs of the company?

8. What is the salary range for this job?

Employment Agencies

State agencies   The government has its own employment agencies. They keep listings of available job openings and try to provide applicants with job leads. Studies show that about 60 percent of the people who use government agencies find employment through them. Government agencies include state Departments of Employment Security and J.T.P.A., or Job Training Partnership agencies. Their services may include job counseling, resume and letter services, and sometimes subsidies for child care and transportation.

Private agencies There are over 8,000 private employment agencies in the United States. Many specialize in finding people for financial, data processing, health care, office, or communications jobs. Private agencies place only 4 percent of those entering the job market and 15 percent of Americans changing jobs. Some charge the applicant a fee for their services; some charge the fee to the employer.

Pointers
1. Ask employers you would like to work for which agencies they use. Find out the names of the most competent people at those agencies. Then call that agency and counselor and tell them you were referred by the firm from which you got their name.

2. Try to find agencies that specialize in your career area: clerical, mechanical, sales, or whatever. Look for their ads in industry magazines and the Yellow Pages.

3. Fees can be paid by the employer, the applicant (you), or a combination of both. Some fees are negotiated at the time the hiring decision is made. Some fees are high, though; so be sure to find out. Agencies are required by law to give you written notice of their fees before you make your agreement. *If the fee is too high, don't sign.* Go to a different agency.

4. Beware of clauses in contracts that require you to pay a fee if you should leave a job within 30 days.

5. You can work with three or four agencies in different parts of the country at the same time. Do not sign up with two agencies that would perform the same services for you in the same area.

6. Follow the advice the counselors give you regarding your resume, your appearance, and interviewing techniques. Check with your counselor every few days to see what is being done.

School Placement Offices Most college and trade school placement offices offer some of the following services:

- Vocational testing of interest and aptitude
- Current job openings

- Reference books, professional journals, business directories, and employer information (annual reports, product information, job descriptions)
- Career development courses, workshops, job fairs.

Even if you never attended the school near your home, try to take advantage of their services.

Rank the three job search methods that would be best for you, by numbering them 1, 2, and 3 below.

_____ Apply directly to employer.

_____ Ask friends or relatives.

_____ Answer newspaper ads.

_____ Use private employment agencies.

_____ Use state employment services.

_____ Use school placement offices.

_____ Place newspaper ads.

_____ Answer ads in professional or trade journals.

Resumes, Applications, and Cover Letters
23

A Step-by-Step Guide for Resume Preparation

Your resume (pronounced REZ-oo-may) is your advertisement for yourself. The resume is the basic door-opener for most careers. The resume accompanies letters of application to employers and is left with them after interviews as a reminder of your qualifications. It introduces you to an employer and advertises your most important skills, abilities, and accomplishments. Your resume should "package" your qualifications in an appealing wrapper that an employer will not pass up.

What should be in a resume:

- Identification section—Who you are
- Job objective section—What you want to do
- Background section—What you have to offer in the way of education, skills, personal experience, and accomplishments

Resumes may take two different formats: chronological and functional.

Chronological Resume Format

Name Address Phone number (Include area code)	Personal information. Some experts advise specifying marital status, height, weight, and health, but the majority feel the disadvantages outweigh the advantages and suggest omitting personal information.
JOB OBJECTIVE	A brief statement indicating position sought and type of organization preferred. (Include only if the same objective can be used for all applications.)
EDUCATION	Name institutions and dates attended in reverse chronological order. Include all learning experiences after high school: military training, on-the-job training, college equivalency programs, and college work. List the schools attended, the dates enrolled, degrees earned, certificates or licenses, and dates they were awarded. Make note of significant honors, scholarships, and extracurricular participation. Put down your major field and overall grade point average if these are to your advantage.
WORK EXPERIENCE	List names and locations of former employers in reverse chronological order. Include titles and positions held, major responsibilities, skills and accomplishments. Omit or group together work experience that bears little relationship to the type of work you are seeking.
MILITARY OBLIGATION	If applicable, summarize military experience and show draft classification.
MISCELLANEOUS INFORMATION	Describe any relevant points not covered elsewhere in your resume: school honors, organization memberships, travel experience, foreign language expertise, outside interests.
REFERENCES	References will be furnished upon request. Do not list references on the resume. This will enable you to have a flexible list of references that can be used as needed.

Rules for Resume Writing

1. Write short, concise sentences. Use as few words as necessary to express your accomplishments.

2. Use action verbs to begin each sentence or phrase.

Examples: created, exhibited, mobilized, repaired, designed, motivated, presented.

3. Use the vocabulary or "jargon" of your field, but avoid becoming overly technical. Speak a language the person reading the resume will understand.

4. List specific accomplishments and results. Use numbers when possible.
   - Increased production by 25 percent.
   - Devised sales campaign that netted $1,500 for class treasury.
   - Won *Atlantic Monthly* national short story writing contest.

5. Convey one selling point at a time. Don't confuse your accomplishments by grouping too many ideas together.

6. Put the concerns of your potential employer ahead of your own needs. This may mean rewriting your resume several times in order to focus on various aspects of your accomplishments.

7. Don't get too personal. No one usually cares that you do needlework or collect trains. Do not include your picture on the resume unless you are applying for work in a field like modeling or acting where physical appearance is part of the job itself.

8. Type the resume in a clear, clean typeface. Commercial typing or word-processing services can do the final typing. The layout should look professional and entice people to read it. Retain sufficient white space, leaving at least one-inch margins, and double space between paragraphs.

9. Fit your resume on one page of 8½-by-11-inch paper. Employers receive many resumes each week and often spend as little as 15 seconds on each one.

10. Even if you use a software program on a computer that checks your spelling, have someone proofread your final copy for any errors.

11. Have the resume professionally printed or duplicated (photo-offset is best). Select off-white, beige, or light gray paper, and use a heavy grade quality. Buy from the printer matching envelopes and blank pieces of paper for writing cover letters.

Resume Strategy No. 1: Taking Inventory

In the highly competitive job market of the 1990s, you become your own advertising manager. Your task is to sell yourself. Any good sales campaign begins with an inventory of selling points.

List all learning experiences, including military training, on-the-job training, and college equivalency programs in which you have participated. If you went to college, list the dates enrolled, any degrees earned, and the dates they were awarded. List any full-time work experience here, beginning with your current job and listing the jobs backwards.

Resume Strategy No. 2: Accomplishment Inventory

The following exercise lists action verbs. Use them to create phrases that explain your accomplishments. Try to think of things you have done in which you have performed one of the actions listed.

Produced _____

Managed _____

Developed _____

Created _____

Expanded _____

Supervised _____

Organized _____

Operated _____

Designed _____

Improved _____

Conducted _____

Administered _____

Established _____

Analyzed _____

Invented _____

Evaluated _____

Exhibited _____

Achieved _____

Reorganized _____

Sold _____

Presented _____

Delivered _____

Resume Strategy No.3: Composing Your Career Objective

To formulate a career objective, begin by defining your strongest skill areas. List four accomplishments, things that made you proud. Begin the list with a series of action words. Here is a list of action words that could be used to begin each sentence:

edited	generated	surveyed	developed	supervised
led	earned	planned	handled	read
organized	won	conducted	revised	persuaded
presided	sold	wrote	coordinated	taught

Accomplishments	Talent or Skills
(sample) Achieved balanced budget for club banquet.	good planner, leadership abilities
1.	
2.	
3.	
4.	

Now ask yourself, "What qualities or abilities do I have that enable me to do this? In the column to the right, summarize the skills or inborn abilities that enabled you to make each of these accomplishments.

Name two positions you would like to seek:_____

Now name two skills which you believe you have and which would be needed in these careers:_____

Now try to compose a job objective. It can be phrased something like this:

I would like to use my _____ and _____

skills in a _____

or _____ position.

Resume Strategy No. 4: Composing the First Draft

Name:
Address:
City & State:
Phone:
JOB OBJECTIVE:

I would like to use my _____ and _____

skills in a _____ or _____
position.

EDUCATION:

_____
_____
_____
_____
_____

MILITARY STATUS:

_____

WORK EXPERIENCE:

_____
_____
_____
_____
_____
_____
_____

REFERENCES AVAILABLE UPON REQUEST.

Resume Strategy No. 5: Critique Your Resume

Always have some competent person proofread and evaluate your resume before duplicating it. Here is an evaluation form to help in making concrete suggestions for improvement.

Resume Checklist	Suggestions for Improvement
Does the overall appearance make you want to read the resume?	
Are there any typos or misspellings?	
Are the margins clear and consistent?	
Could the layout be improved?	
Is the resume well typed on one page?	
Is there any irrelevant information?	
Could the resume be shortened?	
Are all periods of time accounted for?	
Does the resume begin with the most recent accomplishment?	
Is the writing style clear, concise, and understandable?	
Do action verbs begin each sentence or phrase about accomplishments?	
Does the resume stress skills, accomplishments, and results?	
Is all important information included?	

RESUME

Henry Furner
927 Myra Street #8A
San Francisco, CA 90430
(903) 555-8736

JOB OBJECTIVE: I would like a position relating to restaurant operation in the California area.

EDUCATION:
University of Southern Illinois—Carbondale, IL—Bachelor's in restaurant management, 1984.
Finished in top half of class.
Freeport High School—graduated 1980—college prep track.

EXPERIENCE:
19____-____ Worked and travelled in Europe.
19____-____ Financial Credit Coordinator
            Household Credit Corp. Winnetka, IL
19____-____ Associate Manager
            JoJo's Restaurants Buffalo Grove, IL
19____-____ Credit & Collection Officer and customer service agent
            General Tire Company Elk Grove, IL

CAREER ACCOMPLISHMENTS:
Upgraded customer service standards within a large retail tire company.
Assisted in the design and implementation of a new code of restaurant table service standards.
Established a high volume of "repeat" business for a large consumer finance institution.
Head waiter of a Swiss summer resort and assistant to the manager.

HOBBIES: Jogging, skiing, photography

Miscellaneous: Fluent in French and Italian
                Member of Phi Alpha Theta International Honor Society in History

Resume Strategy No. 6: Selecting References

Employers will check with references to verify statements made on your application regarding salary, length of employment, and your reason for leaving the company. They also want to obtain your previous employers' estimates of your work habits and strong and weak points.

It is best to have more than the required number of references. Use those who know your skills in the areas you want to emphasize most for each job.

List previous employers, teachers, and others who know your skills for at least two references. Pastors or people in the community who can vouch for your personal character may be used for a third.

Always get the permission of the person you list as a reference. References are typed on a separate sheet of paper and given to an employer when requested.

Question

Sue applied for a position at a large company and was informed that the company would run a character check on her. Having nothing to hide, she gave her permission. She was not offered the job, so she suspects that whoever did the checking discovered something negative about her. Does she have the right to know who said something about her and whether the information was correct?

Answer

Under the Fair Credit Reporting Act, Sue is entitled to find out who did the investigating and what was reported. If the information is false, she has the right to have it corrected. The reporting agency must let the employer know that a mistake was made.

Your References

Name _____

Position _____ Company _____

Address _____ Phone _____

Name _____

Position _____ Company _____

Address _____ Phone _____

Correspondence That Wins Interviews

Never mail your resume to any employer without writing a personalized cover letter. Here is a sample newspaper ad and responding cover letter.

> We are a growing, aggressive consumer goods company looking for an experienced Accounting Supervisor to assist in our accounting department. Duties will include supervision of clerks in the areas of inventory, accounts payable, and accounts receivable.
>
> We offer good starting salary, insurance benefits and company-paid profit sharing.
>
> Write Irene Kimball, Sr. Accountant
> The Stroup Exchange, Inc.
> 3399 Dundee Rd. N.E.
> Perkins, Iowa 52301

Notice that the ad asks for an experienced worker and that the duties will include supervision of others. Check to see what kinds of work will be handled by the department. Experience in these areas should be mentioned in the cover letter.

At the same time, you should be careful not to overload the letter with details—remember that you will want to have something to say during the interview as well. The resume and the cover letter should give the "big picture" accurately, but should not be so long that the reader loses interest.

Use stationery that matches the size and color of your resume. Off-white, beige, or gray papers are best.

Write to a person who has the power to hire you, using name and title. Always direct your letter to a particular person. Call the company and request a name if none is given in the ad.

Identify the job for which you are applying.

Enumerate the qualifications you have that the employer requires.

State that you will take the initiative in contacting the employer.

Type your letter professionally, limiting it to one page.

Sign your full name. Use a blue pen with a medium felt tip. These pens give a forcefulness that may help.

Donna Burke
809 Crandall Drive
Cedar Rapids, IA 52402
318-555-8995

Ms. Irene Kimball
Senior Accountant
The Stroup Exchange, Inc.
3399 Dundee Rd. N.E.
Perkins, Iowa 52301

Dear Ms. Kimball:

Please consider me for the position advertised in the September 4, 199__ *Chicago Tribune.*

The enclosed resume highlights my educational qualifications to supervise employees and prepare budget reports.

My experience supervising 15 waitresses at Keystone, Colorado, has sharpened my ability to motivate, oversee, and discipline employees in any setting. I have had 30 hours college work in accounting and am familiar with most current reporting methods.

Please expect my call next week. I hope we can meet for an interview.

Sincerely,

Donna Burke

Here are other guidelines for writing effective letters: Keep your letters short and simple. Avoid flowery words; be direct. Keep paragraphs short—no more than 5 or 6 lines each. Double spacing between paragraphs adds to readability.

Application Forms

Complete any application form as neatly as possible. If it is sloppy, it suggests that you are impatient or inattentive to detail. If it is neat and complete, it suggests that you are methodical, patient, and detail-oriented.

Use only black or blue pen. Your pen should let you print neatly without blobs, smudges, or smears. A fine-point makes it easier to print small. Avoid erasures and cross-outs; they indicate concern or anxiety about the topic.

Read the instructions before writing anything on an application. Many applications begin with general instructions, such as "Print in ink" or "Type." Since employers want to hire people who can follow instructions on the job, the way you follow directions on the application gives an indication of what kind of employee you might be.

If an application question does not apply to you, make a short dash (—). If an honest answer to a question might screen you out of the job, leave it blank or write "will explain on interview." Never admit anything negative about yourself without the opportunity to give an explanation.

Name

List your name just as it is asked for on an application. Application forms usually ask for last name first, then first name, then middle initial. Do not use nicknames unless there is a special blank for it. You want to show that you are businesslike, so use your complete legal name. Most applications require a signature at the end. Sign your name in the same form as you use to sign checks or legal papers.

Address

All applications ask for your current address. Some ask for previous addresses or your permanent address. Be prepared with house numbers and zip codes.

Date of birth

Date of birth and age can only be asked before hiring to satisfy minimum age requirements. Answer this question if you are a minor or might appear under age. Put a dash if you are obviously a mature adult.

Telephone number

Since many employers contact job applicants by phone, it is important that you list a phone number with an answering machine or one that is likely to be answered during the day. If no one can answer your phone, and you don't have an answering machine, then list the number of someone reliable who can accept your message.

If the number is an office with an extension, include the extension number. It is also a good idea to list two numbers so that if the first number is unanswered, people can try the second.

Social security number — Be sure you have your correct number and list it legibly. If you do not have a social security number, apply for one at your social security or post office.

Position sought — You should know what you want to do. If you respond "any job," you won't make a strong impression. List the title of the job you want and then put in parentheses "or similar position." This shows that you have a specific goal but are open to other possibilities. If you do not know the job title, check with the librarian at the public library, a career counselor, union official, or other person who will be familiar with the job area that interests you. If you have had a job, it is best if you apply for a job that represents a step forward.

Salary expected — The best response to salary queries is "Open." You then don't commit yourself to a figure that is too high or too low. When interviewing, you should know the market value of the position. Salaries are computed by hour, week, two-week period, month, or year. Compute your desired salary in terms of each pay period.

Education — Most applications ask detailed questions about your education, so be prepared with schools you attended and the dates you were enrolled. If there is not enough space, list only the schools from which you graduated.

When asked about further schooling, list the courses that would benefit you in the career you want. Leave future schooling blank if you are not sure of your goals. If asked how your education was financed, list the percentage of tuition and expenses that you earned. For example, "Earned 25 percent of college tuition and expenses."

Activities — Many applications provide a special, separate section for volunteer activities. Volunteer work can develop important skills and responsibility. If there is no special section for volunteer work, list it under Work Experience.

Previous employment — Employers find this section extremely important. Be prepared with names and addresses of former employers. List your present job first and move back in time. If you have no work experience, leave this section blank. Between the education section and the work experience section, all years should be explained. Under "reason for leaving," make positive statements about yourself and your goals rather than being negative about your former employers. In other words, say "desired more responsibility" rather than "boss was very hard to get along with."

Remember when answering questions about future plans that employers want to hire people who will stay with the company. Answer such questions with a response, "as long as my skills are being fully used" if that can honestly be said.

Be sure that all times are accounted for, as gaps in an application can indicate that you are trying to cover up something negative.

Military status — Most applications ask about military background. If you were honorably discharged, list all the data. If you received less than an honorable discharge, leave the section blank. Be prepared to discuss your military experience in the interview. Put a dash if you were never in the service, registered for the draft, or in reserves.

References — A reference is a person who will testify to your character and abilities as an employee. Employers often contact references, so list them carefully; always ask permission before listing anyone as a reference. People commonly used for references include former employers, supervisors and co-workers, former teachers, friends who have jobs indicating responsibility, and people who have known you in a volunteer capacity. Family members should not be listed.

Be prepared with names, addresses, and phone numbers of three people who have agreed to provide references.

The Interview

24

The interview is the single most important step in winning the employment game. The interview is your chance to determine if you would like to work for an employer and the employer's chance to determine your suitability for a job. Too many interviews are psychological games, parent-child confrontations where the interviewer (the parent) asks questions of the prospective employee (the child). Think of the interview as a negotiation where the basic issues are: What do I want? What do you want? How can we both get what we want?

Interview Strategy No. 1: Winning Interviews

After an employer has received your resume, you should telephone to schedule an interview. Your call should have a definite opening, middle, and conclusion.

Have a pen or pencil and paper ready. Telephone from a quiet place. Try not to use a pay telephone. Ask for the person it is best to speak with—the person who has the power to hire you.

State who you are, that you sent a letter and resume, and why you are qualified for the job you seek. Set up a meeting at which your employment could be discussed. Write down the details of the interview: name of interviewer; date and time; address and room number; travelling directions, if needed.

Dealing with Secretaries

Ask directly for the person you want.	This is Edward Lopez. May I speak with Mr. Chung?"
	"What is this in reference to?"
State your purpose.	"I would like to discuss the landscaping position you have open."
	"Perhaps I can help you."
If you can't get through, try to get an appointment.	"Yes, could I arrange a meeting with Mr. Chung to discuss this position early next week?"
	"Mr. Chung's schedule is filled for next week."
Try again to get an appointment.	"Then, when would be a good time for me to call back to speak with him? He has received my resume and I'm anxious to discuss the opening with him."
	"Mr. Chung will contact you if he is interested in your resume."

Try to avoid the secretary if he or she is a zealous gatekeeper. Call back before 8:30, at lunchtime, or after 5:00. Many bosses work long days, while their secretaries leave on time.

Keep a record of your telephone contacts. Write down the name of the company, the person(s) with whom you talk, and the results. A sample record form is supplied on the next page.

Telephone Contact Form

Company's name _____

Contact person _____

Job I seek _____

My special qualifications to hold that job _____

_____

Results of telephone call _____

_____

- -

Company's name _____

Contact person _____

Job I seek _____

My special qualifications to hold that job _____

_____

Results of telephone call _____

_____

- -

Company's name _____

Contact person _____

Job I seek _____

My special qualifications to hold that job _____

_____

Results of telephone call _____

_____

Your Legal Rights

Knowing your rights means knowing the law.

It is the law that when applying for a job you cannot be discriminated against because of race, color, religion, sex, age, or in many cases, certain physical or mental handicaps.

Employers interpret anti-bias laws differently and may ask questions that could be discriminatory. Knowing what can be asked legitimately in interviews and applications can protect your rights.

Interview Strategy No. 2: Know Your Rights

To be comfortable in an interview, it is helpful to understand the rights and responsibilities of both the applicant and the employer.

Rights and Responsibilities of Employer

- To establish lines of communication, make you feel comfortable.
- To evaluate your appearance and personal demeanor.
- To evaluate the relevancy of your education to the job.
- To understand your work experience.
- To explain the responsibilities of the job opening.
- To explain company benefits, vacation policies.
- To notify you when a decision will be made on the opening.
- To determine your interest in the job.
- To administer any tests relating to the job.
- To assess your suitability for the job.
- To negotiate acceptable salary.

Rights and Responsibilities of Applicant

- To highlight aspects of your education that best reveal your abilities and background.
- To communicate the achievements of your past life, whether it be work or volunteer activity.
- To communicate a sincere interest by asking knowledgeable questions about the position.
- To discover what future or career path may result if you accept this position.
- To negotiate a fair and acceptable salary.
- To reach an understanding of the duties and rewards associated with the position.
- To persuade the employer to hire you.
- To determine the employer's interest in you.
- To establish basis for continuing communication.

What Questions Can an Employer Legally Ask?

	Acceptable Question	Unacceptable Question
Name	What names or nicknames have you used in your past work?	What is your maiden name? What is your original name?
Address and Phone	What is your address? Phone number? How long have you resided in the city and state where the employer is located? If you have no phone, where can we reach you?	Do you rent or own your own home? What is your birthplace? What is the birthplace of your parents, spouse, or relatives?
Creed or Religion		What is your religion? What church do you attend? What religious holidays do you observe?
Appearance	What general distinguishing physical characteristics (such as scars) do you have? Height may be requested only when it is a bona fide occupational requirement.	What is the color of your hair, eyes, skin? What is your weight? (Photographs may be required *after* hiring.)
Age	Can you furnish proof of age if you are hired? Date of birth may be needed to: (1) maintain apprenticeship requirements (2) satisfy state or federal minimum age statutes (3) administer retirement, pension, or employee benefits	What is the date of your birth? What is your age?
Education	What schools did you attend? What degrees were earned? What academic work is in progress? What vocational training have you had on your own or through an employer?	What year did you graduate from high school? Grade school? College?

	Acceptable Question	**Unacceptable Question**
Citizenship	Are you a U.S. citizen? Do you have the legal right to work in the U.S.?	Are you a naturalized or native-born citizen? Do you intend to become a citizen? Of what country are you a citizen?
National Origin		What is your ancestry? What is the nationality of your parents or spouse? (Unless the employer is an organization promoting a particular national heritage.)
Language	What languages do you speak or write fluently?	What is your native tongue? What language is spoken in your home? How did you acquire fluency in another language?
Relatives and Dependents	What relatives are already employed by this company? Name and address of person to be notified in case of emergency.	Do you have any children? If so, how old are they? Who lives in your household? What child care provisions do you have?
Marital Status		Do you want to be addressed as Mrs., Miss, or Ms.? Are you married? Divorced? Widowed? Single?
Military Experience	Are you a veteran? Did the military provide you with job training? Have you been notified to report for duty in the armed forces?	What foreign military experience have you had? Some states forbid questions such as: Are you eligible for military service? What were the dates and conditions of your discharge?
Organizations	To what union, trade, or professional societies do you belong?	What clubs or organizations do you belong to?

	Acceptable Question	**Unacceptable Question**
References	Names and addresses of persons willing to provide professional or character references? Who suggested that you apply? Do you have any objections if we check your employer for references?	Who is your pastor or religious leader?
Arrest Record	How many times have you been convicted of a felony? What were you convicted for?	Have you ever been arrested?
Health and Handicaps	Do you have any physical or mental impairments that could prevent you from performing on this job? Are there any duties you could not perform because of health reasons?	
Financial Status		Have your wages ever been attached or garnisheed?
Employment History	How many years of experience do you have? What are the names and addresses of previous employers? What were your duties? How long did you hold the job? Why did you leave your previous job? Why do you seek this position?	

Assertive Interviewing Techniques

Communicating honestly, directly, and in an appropriate way is vital for winning the employment game. What you say, the tone of your voice, even your posture can communicate your basic self-respect. Unfortunately, interviewers do not always act within the law, and it is necessary to assert your rights to win good employment.

Some people are assertive, some nonassertive, some aggressive. The most successful people are assertive. Recognizing the difference between these types of behavior can make assertiveness easier to master.

Nonassertive behavior

Nonassertive people may violate their own rights by failing to express their feelings, thoughts, and beliefs. Their actions may seem apologetic or self-effacing, and others may perceive them as weak or lacking in self-esteem because they do not speak up for themselves.

Assertive behavior

Assertive people believe in their basic human rights. They approach others as human beings, not adversaries. They stand up for their rights, needs, desires, and beliefs. They articulate their thoughts honestly and directly without violating other people's rights. An assertive person communicates, "I will stand up for my own rights without violating yours."

Aggressive behavior

Aggressive people stand up for their rights, desires, feelings, and beliefs but attack others, violating the rights of other people. They dominate to get their points across. Their message says, "I must win; you're unimportant. This is what I feel; your feelings don't count. This is what I think; you're stupid for believing differently."

Check Your Body Language

We can communicate as much with body language as with speech. Below are some examples to help you determine whether your body language is assertive. Mark each example either *S* or *I,* after you have thought over the response each action would bring.

S: Satisfactory. Behavior is assertive.
I: Improvement needed. Behavior is nonassertive or aggressive.

____Using direct eye contact

____Blinking rapidly

____Having open, relaxed facial expression

____Emphasizing key words

____Maintaining well-balanced posture

____Biting lips

____Using relaxed demeanor

____Gesturing to emphasize key points

____Using bored expression

____Wrinkling forehead

____Being tight-lipped

____Having clenched teeth

____Whining

____Speaking loudly

____Nodding excessively

____Using a condescending manner

____Keeping hands on hips

____Keeping eyes downcast

____Smiling inappropriately

____Using firm voice

____Laughing inappropriately

____Wetting lips

____Staring into the distance

____Clearing throat

____Speaking too softly

____Speaking rapidly

____Covering mouth when speaking

____Fiddling with glasses, jewelry

____Pounding fists

____Pointing finger

Investigate the Employer

The more prepared you are for an interview, the more likely that you will win the employment game. Many employers reject applicants because they show little interest or enthusiasm for the company.

Thoroughly research every company with which you interview. Possible sources for finding out about any organization include:

- Leaflets, brochures, and annual reports published by the company
- Advertisements for its products
- Job description for the job you are seeking
- Employees of the organization
- Trade journals and magazines found in libraries
- The local Chamber of Commerce
- Customers who use the company's products
- The local library's files of newspapers and clippings
- Business directories to be found in library
- The local Better Business Bureau
- Dun & Bradstreet ratings
- Stock market performance, if available

If the company that you are interested in has recently built new additions, or has purchased land, and is building new factories or offices, you may be able to find articles in back issues of newspapers in the area, which will tell what the expansion will be. This is a good source of advance information about possible jobs. Even though a company has not advertised for applicants, you can assume that if they are building new additions they will need at least some new employees at the new location.

If, on the other hand, the organization is moving to smaller, less desirable quarters, or employees have been recently laid off, you should be cautious. If the company is not financially stable, you need to look elsewhere.

In most cases your research should reveal financial and organizational stability. Then you can concentrate on the positive reasons for employer research. Is the major work of the organization the kind to which you can give your whole-hearted efforts? Will the environment be a good one for your occupational growth? Do you have skills and talents to offer this kind of organization? Does the organization have the rewards you want in return?

Employer Inventory

Company: _____

Address: _____

Phone: _____

Contact Person: _____

Skills that should be emphasized with this employer: _____
_____

Deficiencies in my background that this employer may have reservations about:
_____
_____

How I can overcome these deficiencies: _____
_____

Company: _____

Address: _____

Phone: _____

Contact Person: _____

Skills that should be emphasized with this employer: _____
_____

Deficiencies in my background that this employer may have reservations about:
_____
_____

How I can overcome these deficiencies: _____
_____

Rehearsing the Interview

In order to see yourself as others see you, try role playing an interview as though you were an actor on stage. Role playing can help to put you at ease with potential interview situations and will prepare you to answer many questions.

Levels of role play

1. Role play alone with the aid of a mirror. Sit in front of the mirror. Ask yourself questions and answer them. Speak aloud in a firm, clear voice, answering your own questions. Watch yourself as you speak. Is your voice trembling? Are there any nervous gestures? If you have any nervous gestures, try folding your hands in your lap, folding them on a table. Keep working until you sound and appear self-assured, calm, and knowledgeable about your background and potential.

2. Tape record an interview. Involve friends as the interviewers and try to get their feedback on how you sound.

3. If available use a videotape recorder and tape yourself in a mock interview. Video equipment is becoming readily available through schools and professional organizations. Get a friend to act as the interviewer and to critique your performance.

4. Ask your friend to create an ad for an employee for her or his imaginary organization. Have your friend write down the "information" about the employer that you might find out during an "employer inventory." Then role play the mock interview as though this were all you knew about the organization. Use the facts of your own real work history, and try to convince your friend to hire you.

The Questions Behind the Questions

Many of the same questions are asked of applicants again and again. The questions focus on four basic areas:

- Personality
- Personal interests
- Educational history
- Employment history

Here are some questions that could make the difference between getting the job you want and settling for a disappointing second choice.

Your personality

Question
Describe yourself as a worker.

Translation
Can you get along with others?

More people are fired because they cannot get along with others than because they lack job skills. When answering this type of question, focus on your interpersonal abilities. Try to picture yourself on the job. Which of your personal qualities would make you the best person to perform those duties? Employers are attracted toward people who are willing to work hard, but tend to avoid the workaholic.

Question
Describe your greatest weaknesses/strengths.

Translation
Are you realistic and capable of assessing your work habits?

Be honest in your assessments. Try to show how you are working on turning your weaknesses into strengths.

Question
Tell me about yourself.

Translation
I didn't read your resume carefully.

Briefly go over your background, leaving out personal details.

Question
What can you contribute to our company?

Translation
Sell yourself.

Briefly review your strong points as an employee, noting past job experience and education that will help you on the new job.

Your employment history and expectations

Question
Which of your jobs did you like best? What motivates you?

Translation
What makes you work best?

Is it salary, benefits, seasonal work that allows you time off? The chance to be creative? The chance to learn on a job? Answer this question with the employer's viewpoint in mind. In describing past jobs you enjoyed, pick those that are most closely related to the job opening. Stress what you can do for the employer, rather than salary or benefits you expect.

Question
What do you expect to be doing five years from now?

Translation
How long do you expect to be with this company?

Employers want to hire people with long-term potential. Let the employer know that you expect to remain in the industry, if that is a truthful answer. You might also want to indicate that you would like to assume more responsibility as the years go by.

Question
Are you willing to relocate? Travel? Work overtime?

Translation
Will your family commitments interfere with the job? How willing are you to get ahead?

Let the employer know that you are flexible, but set realistic limits on your availability.

Rehearse any problem areas

On a separate sheet of paper, list some questions you would not want to be asked in an interview. Then think carefully about how you can answer the questions honestly, but without getting into areas you don't want to discuss. Write out the ways you would prefer to answer if the questions ever come up in an interview.

Winning the Salary Game

Some questions about salary negotiation:

Q: How do I establish a realistic salary range?
A: Thoroughly check newspapers, trade journals, private employment agencies, state employment offices, com-

panies employing workers with your skills, professional trade associations, and executive recruiters. From your research decide on three figures:

Aspiration level: What is the highest salary you could earn?

Midrange figure: What would you accept after making some concessions?

Bottom line: What is the lowest salary you would accept for a job?

Q: At what point in the interview process should salary be discussed?
A: Don't discuss salary until you are certain you have a firm job offer.

Q: How do I avoid naming too low a figure?
A: Let the employer state a salary range first. Ask something like, "This position sounds like one which would put my abilities to good use. What is the salary range?"

Q: How do I sell my services for the highest price?
A: Be prepared to emphasize your accomplishments, not your needs. Do not hesitate to restate selling points about yourself that you made earlier. Be prepared with concrete evidence of your productivity. If the employer balks at your expectations, try to negotiate a salary review at the end of six months.

Q: How important are fringe benefits? Can good benefits substitute for salary?
A: There are many benefits that can substitute for salary. They include: travel benefits like those airline employees receive, goods at a discount, extra insurance plans or dental coverage, educational assistance, profit sharing or stock options, reduced-interest loans, and company cars.

Winning Interview Strategies

You are punctual. You check ahead to be sure you know how to get there. If the personnel office is part of a larger complex or in a sizable office building you arrive at the main entrance 15 minutes before the hour of your appointment.

You act naturally and courteously.

You dress in businesslike clothing. As a guideline you ask yourself, "What do successful people in this line of work wear?" and dress accordingly.

Losing Interview Strategies

You show no interest in the organization.

You cannot express yourself clearly.

You use poor grammar.

You want to start at the top.

You have no career commitment, evident purpose in life.

You are unwilling to consider additional training in new skill areas.

You act cynical, intolerant.

You have a sloppy personal appearance.

Winning Interview Strategies

You listen to the questions carefully. Taking a few seconds to think about your answer, you answer clearly and concisely. You do not exaggerate your abilities or experience.

You respond to all questions. If it is to your advantage, you volunteer information which might concern the interviewer but cannot be legally asked.

You remember to use the names of the interviewers. You rivet your attention to every introduction. If you don't catch the name, you ask that it be repeated. You use the names as you answer the questions.

You maintain a posture of interest. You try to establish eye contact with the interviewer as this implies sincerity.

You are prepared with questions about the job and the company that you are entitled to know: salary range, responsibilities, benefits, supervision and evaluation policies, advancement opportunities.

You are prepared with credentials and references. You have checked the names, addresses, and phone numbers of former employers and references are spelled correctly and are up-to-date.

You show serious interest in the job. You are enthusiastic and self-confident.

You do not criticize yourself or other people.

You avoid emotional answers or wisecracks.

You do not smoke.

You thank the interviewer at the end of the interview, and send a written thank-you within the next few days.

Losing Interview Strategies

You act overly aggressive, pushy, conceited.

You put down your last bosses.

You are evasive about your past work record.

You have poor body language, lack of eye contact with the interviewer, a weak handshake, slumpy posture.

You act nervous, gesture frequently.

You act negative about school.

You lack a sense of humor.

Your mind wanders as you listen to the questions being asked. You answer in a vague way and mumble when you are unsure that you are answering correctly. You do not even try to figure out whether the interviewer has understood what you have said.

You have not brought along any information that you need about former employers, their addresses or telephone numbers. You have to ask for a telephone directory to fill out the forms, and then you leave it lying carelessly where you used it without bothering to return it to its place.

You show that you know nothing whatever about the company by looking startled and saying, "Oh, do you make electrical insulators? I didn't know that! What else do you make?"

You hold up the interviewer from other work that he or she has to do and continue to ask questions after the person has already indicated that the interview is over. This mistake is especially bad if the questions and your ongoing conversation have nothing whatever to do with the interview or anything of interest to the interviewer.

You fail to thank the interviewer.

Checklist for Winning the Employment Game 25

Put a check as you actually fulfill steps to gaining full employment.

_____ You use a variety of job search methods.

_____ Apply directly to employer.

_____ Ask friends or relatives for job leads.

_____ Answer newspaper ads.

_____ Register with private employment agency.

_____ Register with state employment agency.

_____ Check with school placement offices.

_____ Place newspaper ad.

_____ Answer ads in professional or trade journals.

_____ You follow the step-by-step guide for resume preparation.

_____ You get permission from the people you wish to list as references.

_____ You write a customized cover letter for each resume that you mail out.

_____ You use follow-up telephone calls to gain interviews.

_____ You role-play the interview.

_____ You research the salary range you can legitimately expect.

_____ You research each company before you interview there.

_____ You arrive for interviews punctually.

_____ You dress appropriately for the interview.

_____ You remember the name of the interviewer.

_____ You answer all questions assertively and clearly.

Remember that you are changing from time to time and that the job requirements in the world are changing, too. At the same time that you may be experiencing a growing interest in the environment and in ecology, the world may be developing a growing need for people to work in these areas, also.

From time to time, you will want to assess your skills and the state of the job market. If you have new interests, you will want to develop some new skills to help you move into new areas. Whenever you feel the need to reassess your job potential, or your career goals, you will want to revamp your career plans.

At times of change in your career goals, you will follow the same steps that you have followed in using this workbook, and in working with your career guidance advisor in school or in another service organization. You may want to use the actual forms that appear in this book, and you may want to add to them the personal techniques that you have developed for yourself.

Career Planning in a Changing World 26

If you are approaching a time of great changes in other areas of your life, you will want to do a very thorough job of making the most of your job potential in changing careers. For instance, if you want to change jobs at midlife, you will want to consider that a job may mean different things to you than it did when you were in your twenties. For a person of forty or fifty, perhaps the job will have to take the place of a lot of the home life that occupied the person's time when there were children at home.

Later on, there may come a time when you will want to make a job change at the usual age when many people consider retirement. Perhaps that will be just the time that you will want to pursue a hobby that can be turned into a part- or full-time job. Perhaps you know someone of sixty-five or so who has always wanted to be a ceramics instructor, and now that the person has reached retirement age it is possible to do just that.

Many life changes will bring with them changes in your job needs. An athlete may become disabled and not be able to make a living at sports, but may discover a talent for sales and management. A young couple with small children may find an increasing need for money, in excess of the amounts they originally planned when they chose their careers. Inflation, recessions, military service, and other external conditions of life may intervene to cause your plans to change all through your life. Don't let it throw you; use it to your advantage, and make the time of change a time of growth for your own good. It can be done.

Life Changes That Can Affect Career and Life Planning

Listed below are a number of changes that could occur within a normal life span. Any of these changes might cause a need for further examination and changes in life planning. Read through this list, and consider which changes could take place in your own life. Use the lines provided on the next page to write in additional changes that you can imagine possibly occurring in your own life. Try to estimate when such changes might occur, and consider how they would affect your life and career plans at that time.

- Money problems that make more income essential.
- Marriage and the birth of children.
- The death of a loved one or family member.
- Illness in the family that necessitates someone staying at home with the patient.
- A move to a new town where the industries or businesses are different.
- A technological development that does away with an accustomed job.
- An economic downturn that makes an employer shut down the business.
- The development of an ulcer or other digestive problem that requires a less stressful work environment.
- The shutdown of an industry that has supported the town where you live.
- You have always "messed around" with a hobby. You discover it can bring in more money than the job you have been working at for several years.

- Your parents are elderly and could use some help. They live in another city where most jobs are in the electronics industry.

Additional Changes in Your Own Life

Related Reading

What Color Is Your Parachute? Richard Nelson Bolles, Ten Speed Press, Berkley, 1991.

How to Land a Better Job, Catherine S. Lott and Oscar C. Lott, NTC Publishing Group, Lincolnwood, Illinois, 1989.

Getting a Job in Today's Competitive Market, Adele Lewis and William Lewis, Barron's Educational Series, Woodbury, New York, 1982.

Jobs of the Future, Marvin J. Cetron with Marcia Appel, McGraw-Hill Book Company, New York, 1984.

Where the Jobs Are, William J. McBurney, Jr., Chilton Book Company, Radnor, Pennsylvania, 1982.

Joyce Lain Kennedy's Career Book, Joyce Lain Kennedy and Darryl Laramore, NTC Publishing Group, Lincolnwood, Illinois, 1988.

Occupational Outlook Handbook, U.S. Department of Labor, NTC Publishing Group, Lincolnwood, Illinois, published every two years.

VGM CAREER BOOKS

BUSINESS PORTRAITS
Boeing
Coca-Cola
Ford
McDonald's

CAREER DIRECTORIES
Careers Encyclopedia
Dictionary of Occupational Titles
Occupational Outlook Handbook

CAREERS FOR
Animal Lovers; Bookworms; Caring People; Computer Buffs; Crafty People; Culture Lovers; Environmental Types; Fashion Plates; Film Buffs; Foreign Language Aficionados; Good Samaritans; Gourmets; Health Nuts; History Buffs; Kids at Heart; Music Lovers; Mystery Buffs; Nature Lovers; Night Owls; Number Crunchers; Plant Lovers; Shutterbugs; Sports Nuts; Travel Buffs; Writers

CAREERS IN
Accounting; Advertising; Business; Child Care; Communications; Computers; Education; Engineering; the Environment; Finance; Government; Health Care; High Tech; Horticulture & Botany; International Business; Journalism; Law; Marketing; Medicine; Science; Social & Rehabilitation Services

CAREER PLANNING
Beating Job Burnout
Beginning Entrepreneur
Big Book of Jobs
Career Planning & Development for College Students & Recent Graduates
Career Change
Career Success for People with Physical Disabilities
Careers Checklists
College and Career Success for Students with Learning Disabilities
Complete Guide to Career Etiquette
Cover Letters They Don't Forget
Dr. Job's Complete Career Guide
Executive Job Search Strategies
Guide to Basic Cover Letter Writing
Guide to Basic Résumé Writing
Guide to Internet Job Searching
Guide to Temporary Employment
Job Interviewing for College Students
Joyce Lain Kennedy's Career Book

Out of Uniform
Parent's Crash Course in Career Planning
Slame Dunk Résumés
Up Your Grades: Proven Strategies for Academic Success

CAREER PORTRAITS
Animals; Cars; Computers; Electronics; Fashion; Firefighting; Music; Nature; Nursing; Science; Sports; Teaching; Travel; Writing

GREAT JOBS FOR
Business Majors
Communications Majors
Engineering Majors
English Majors
Foreign Language Majors
History Majors
Psychology Majors
Sociology Majors

HOW TO
Apply to American Colleges and Universities
Approach an Advertising Agency and Walk Away with the Job You Want
Be a Super Sitter
Bounce Back Quickly After Losing Your Job
Change Your Career
Choose the Right Career
Cómo escribir un currículum vitae en inglés que tenga éxito
Find Your New Career Upon Retirement
Get & Keep Your First Job
Get Hired Today
Get into the Right Business School
Get into the Right Law School
Get into the Right Medical School
Get People to Do Things Your Way
Have a Winning Job Interview
Hit the Ground Running in Your New Job
Hold It All Together When You've Lost Your Job
Improve Your Study Skills
Jumpstart a Stalled Career
Land a Better Job
Launch Your Career in TV News
Make the Right Career Moves
Market Your College Degree
Move from College into a Secure Job
Negotiate the Raise You Deserve
Prepare Your Curriculum Vitae

Prepare for College
Run Your Own Home Business
Succeed in Advertising When all You
Succeed in College
Succeed in High School
Take Charge of Your Child's Early Education
Write a Winning Résumé
Write Successful Cover Letters
Write Term Papers & Reports
Write Your College Application Essay

MADE EASY
College Applications
Cover Letters
Getting a Raise
Job Hunting
Job Interviews
Résumés

ON THE JOB: REAL PEOPLE WORKING IN...
Communications
Health Care
Sales & Marketing
Service Businesses

OPPORTUNITIES IN
This extensive series provides detailed information on more than 150 individual career fields.

RÉSUMÉS FOR
Advertising Careers
Architecture and Related Careers
Banking and Financial Careers
Business Management Careers
College Students & Recent Graduates
Communications Careers
Computer Careers
Education Careers
Engineering Careers
Environmental Careers
Ex-Military Personnel
50+ Job Hunters
Government Careers
Health and Medical Careers
High School Graduates
High Tech Careers
Law Careers
Midcareer Job Changes
Nursing Careers
Re-Entering the Job Market
Sales and Marketing Careers
Scientific and Technical Careers
Social Service Careers
The First-Time Job Hunter

VGM Career Horizons
a division of *NTC Publishing Group*
4255 West Touhy Avenue
Lincolnwood, Illinois 60646–1975